Is Anyone Out There Building Mother's Self-Esteem?

Is Anyone Out There Building Mother's Self-Esteem?

MARILYNNE TODD LINFORD

Deseret Book
Salt Lake City, Utah

No part of this book may be reproduced in any
form or by any means without permission in writing
from the publisher, Deseret Book Company,
P.O. Box 30178, Salt Lake City, Utah 84130.
Deseret Book is a registered trademark of
Deseret Book Company, Inc.

First printing September 1986

Library of Congress Cataloging-in-Publication Data

Linford, Marilynne.
    Is anyone out there building mother's self-esteem.

    Includes index.
    1. Spiritual life—Mormon authors.   2. Mothers—
Religious life.   3. Self-respect—Religious aspects—
Christianity.   I. Title.
BX8656.L57 1986   248.4′893320431   86-16657
ISBN 0-87579-048-8

To any mother who ever had a
less than perfect day

Contents

Preface

In 1975 I wanted to write a book for mothers on the fun—joy, if you will—of raising children. My husband and I had five children then; the oldest was eight years old. They were very charming, responsive, intelligent, and beautiful children. Consequently I thought I was a very charming, responsive, intelligent, and beautiful mother. I spent every day practicing my mothering skills. I kept a clean house, read stories to the children, prepared lessons for family home evening, made charts and posters, wrote in my journal, kept our year's supply current, never raised my voice, put loving notes in lunch sacks, and sang as I worked. (This picture may be a bit rosy. Time dulls the memory.)

But now things have changed. I again want to write a book, but not one about the innocent joys of mothering. I want to write a realistic survival course for mothers who suffer different forms of mother abuse from their children and feel overwhelmed by the world. You see, those same five children I described before are now eighteen, seventeen, sixteen, fourteen, and twelve years old. Three more children have joined the family; they are nine, seven, and four years old. And I am ten tired years older.

Instead of writing to instruct, I am writing so as not to destruct. Life now is a billion times more complex than ten years ago. As I watch my friends, family, and fellow sisters in the gospel, I know that I am not alone in my

quest to be an excellent wife and mother, nor am I alone
in the frustrations I meet as I struggle to reach that goal.
So I am writing this book for you *and* for me.

This book will not tell you how to keep a cleaner
house, or how to be more organized, or anything else
that may cause you to feel inadequate, overwhelmed, or
frustrated. My purpose is to talk about how to combat
mother abuse and the pressures of the world. I hope that
as you read this book you will find some ideas to help you
feel better about yourself. We mothers have spent years
learning about how to build the self-esteem of our children. Now it is our turn.

My goal is to help you protect, defend, build, and
maybe even polish your self-esteem. You not only need
light at the end of the tunnel, you need light shining on
today.

ONE

Mother's
Sagging Self-Esteem

Are you the kind of person who cannot wait to know what is going to happen at the end of a book, so you read the last page first? If you are, this book will please you because here, in the very first paragraph, I am going to tell you what the last page of this book says. The complete emphasis of this book is this: every mother needs to take charge of and maintain her own self-esteem. By self-esteem I do not mean self-worth, although it is easy to confuse the two. Self-worth is your value as a human being. You are a child of God and, therefore, are priceless. This is a constant; it never changes. Self-esteem is the way you feel about you. The trick is to get your self-esteem to match your self-worth.

Much has been written about what a mother should do for her children, for her husband, for her home, for the community, and for the Church. I sometimes feel so pulled by each of these forces that I feel like nothing more than a service station. I must keep the station hygienic, pleasing to the eye, and tidy. I must have a constant supply of delectable goodies that fill the air with their fragrance and warm the tummy. I must keep up with the Primary, the PTA, the neighborhood, and the extended family organization. I feel I am expected to keep my home operating like a Fortune 500 corporation. No wonder a mother's feelings about herself sag occasionally.

There is more to a mother's existence than being a service-station operator. What is the key to unlocking our potential that too often stops at mopping the floor? The answer is simple: mother's self-esteem. If I, as a mother, feel good about what I am doing, I can accomplish many things. But if I feel unsuccessful, unloved, and put-upon, my progress is limited and my ability to help others is handicapped. I'm certain that every mother has a sagging self-esteem now and then. That is why each mother needs a plan to help her keep the way she sees herself as healthy as possible. Knowing the causes of low self-esteem is a good place to start.

The Causes

As I've tried to analyze how and why my feelings have evolved from the joy of young motherhood to the frustration, mixed with joy, of middle motherhood (a mother with teenagers), I've finally concluded that there are two contributing reasons: one external and the other internal.

I feel that today's women are a product of the propaganda of the times. I'll never forget an article I read in a woman's magazine a number of years ago. It was entitled "Why Young Mothers Feel Trapped." The magazine had asked any reader (mother) who felt trapped to write in and explain how and why she felt that way. The magazine had fifty thousand responses! I didn't feel trapped. I wouldn't have written in, but a seed was sown: fifty thousand mothers felt trapped, so it was possible that I could feel trapped.

Also, in my efforts to be a perfect mother, I read every child-development book in the public library. (It was a small library.) Although I learned many things about raising children, I found some of the information was a little overwhelming. For example, in an excellent book titled *Dare to Discipline,* author James Dobson states that "the responsibilities of effective parenting are staggeringly heavy at times." This is a true statement, but another seed nested: my responsibilities could be staggeringly heavy.

Then there is the zero-population theory. The theory proposes that each two people have no more than two offspring. Even though I do not agree with this theory, a questioning seed was sown through the comments and actions of others. One day I went shopping in a California grocery store; I was obviously expecting a baby, and I had my two other children with me. The salesclerk took one look at me and said, "You've gotta be crazy. You got yourself a perfect family—a boy and a girl. What did you go and get yourself pregnant for?" That same type of thing happened when I went to a clinic in England for my first visit with my assigned doctor. I was expecting baby number five. The doctor looked over my record and then—in loud, crude, nearly violent terms—told me I had no right to overpopulate the world. He said that if I wouldn't have an abortion then I absolutely must have my tubes tied, and he'd make sure of it. These incidences have long since passed, but still more seeds were planted.

There have been other seeds thrown my way. We've all heard statements like "Get into the real world. Get out of the home. Find fulfillment in life as an individual, not as somebody's mother or wife. Go to work for a change. Do something meaningful. Contribute to society." They are voices calling lo here, lo there; they are temptations to vary from the path of traditional Mormon values where home and family are more important than finding personal achievement at the expense of home and family. These seeds breed discontentment and, if nourished, blossom into dissatisfaction and diminish self-esteem. A mother with poor self-esteem begets both friction in her marriage and children with low self-esteem. These seedlings then grow more and more complicated.

If we combine all of these negative philosophies with the natural problems of raising a family, we will find a situation that is ripe for a generation of mothers who suffer from low self-esteem.

I also believe that many mothers are so engulfed in building their children's self-esteem that they forget to care for their own. No one has written a book for children on how to build their mother's self-esteem. If there were such a book, the children wouldn't read it anyway. If a mother isn't mindful of her own feelings of confidence and self-worth, no one else will be either.

The Fallacies

I attribute my past feelings of disillusionment as a mother to some misleading ideas I held fast to while I was growing up. Perhaps these can be blamed on naiveté, perhaps optimism, perhaps immaturity, but whatever the cause, I had unrealistic expectations of life.

Fallacy one: I believed that once I got married, my husband and I would live happily ever after. Marriage would be a blissful state and children would be a constant joy. I have called this my "Cinderella Syndrome."

Fallacy two: I thought that if I did everything right, nothing would go wrong. I have since learned that it's all right to occasionally lose a library book, dent a fender, have eight children with the flu all at once, sprain my ankle while visiting teaching, forget I was asked to speak in sacrament meeting, and have contention in the home. No one I know has been translated and is not likely to be. Being less than perfect is OK.

Fallacy three: I thought that I was unique in my situation. I thought that no one ever felt as frustrated, unsuccessful, angry, or apprehensive as I did. Everyone else seemed to have it all together; why couldn't I? Slowly, I have come to realize that everyone, every day, basically deals with the same problems. The real strength in life comes in the ability to keep trying. We never fail in trying; we fail only when we don't try.

These three fallacious ideas contributed to my feeling of being overwhelmed, which decreased my self-image. I know now that no one gets married and lives completely happily ever after, that there is opposition in all things, and that everyone has mountains and valleys, problems and successes that are very similar to mine.

TWO

The Cycle
of Mother's Self-Esteem

The cycle of a mother's self-esteem ends most often as it begins—happily. The first minutes of motherhood are often accompanied by a spiritual high. The moments of birth bring tears of joy and feelings of gratitude that surpass any emotion felt before. Having a precious gift from heaven placed in your arms is euphoric.

Soon, the fun and exciting days pass into months. Baby's firsts are recorded in the baby book: first smile, first tooth, first word, first step. Each achievement is also the mother's achievement. She watches with satisfaction and pride. Baby fusses now and then, but his needs are fairly predictable and easy to meet. Baby's first words are "Da-da" and "Ma-ma." His first steps are with outstretched arms to his loving parents. All this builds his mother's love for him, and her self-esteem is healthy in spite of middle-of-the-night feedings. Baby never talks back, never stays out late, never disobeys, and never compares his parents to his friends' parents.

Around the time the child celebrates his second birthday, mother has made a startling discovery. This precious toddler has a mind of his own. He can refuse to eat foods he dislikes, balk at taking naps, or postpone learning what a toilet is for. He also learns that he has some powerful weapons on his side—being so cute and loving are two of his best.

Unless precautions are taken, everything from now

5

on can begin slowly, imperceptibly, to go downhill. Once free agency gets its foot in the door between mother and child, the edge, or maybe wedge, is always there. Most mothers aren't aware of the descent until the child is somewhere near twelve. Suddenly mother could be dealing with a person who is close to her own height and weight. Her child is beginning the natural process of freeing himself from home and parents, which in time will allow marriage and the cycle to begin again. Mother never imagined how little she knew until she grew old enough to have a teenager. Then mother is lucky if she does anything right, or even just OK.

Following is an oversimplified view of a child's life through phrases that are typical of his age. It not only illustrates the cycle of a child's life, but also shows why a mother's self-esteem may suffer during some of these stages.

Age 2: "I wuv you."
Age 3: "You a good cooker, Mommy."
Age 4: "Will you marry me when I get big?"
Age 5: "My mom is the best mom in the whole wide world."
Age 6: "My mom made this for me. Isn't it pretty?"
Age 7: "Please come listen to my prayers and tuck me in."
Age 8: "I belong to a great family who loves me."
Age 9: "My mom will take us. She has nothing else to do."
Age 10: "I like the school's chicken gravy best."
Age 11: "But all my friends have ten-speed bikes."
Age 12: "I'd rather go with Doug's family."
Age 13: "Keep the little kids quiet. They embarrass me."
Age 14: "May I have that when you die?"
Age 15: "You aren't going to wear that are you?"

Age 16: "Did you ever date?"
Age 17: "You just don't understand what it's like
         to be young these days."
Age 18: "How do you ever expect me to get any
         studying done? This place is like a circus."
Age 19: "Mom, you're the greatest! How can I
         thank you for putting up with me all
         these years? I love you."

As you read the typical statements that children make at various stages in their life, it is obvious that they are going through cycles of growth. *You* are also going through cycles of growth. Your cycle is difficult because of the many responsibilities you have and because of the pressures you endure. Part of that pressure exists because your life is involved with many other people's lives. Just remember that you are at least one cycle ahead of your children. Use this advantage to help you maintain your self-esteem. You have already been where they are. You know what it's like to be an infant, a child, a preteen, a teenager, and a newly married bride. The cycle you are now in will also pass. You will not always be the mother of an infant or even a teenager.

Remember that the cycle you are in and the cycle your child is in may not rotate side by side with the precision of watch gears. Your cogs may hit and rub against each other from time to time, so try not to let the actions and words of your children deflate your self-esteem. You are a mother; therefore you have enormous value that cannot be depreciated just because one of your children does not like your chicken gravy!

THREE

How To
Combat Mother Abuse

I define mother abuse as the anxiety, frustration, anger, tension, or trauma—actual or imagined—that children cause in their mothers. Children, knowingly or innocently, use verbal or psychological means that can cause their mothers to feel unsuccessful or inadequate.

How can a child wield such power over his mother? It is because the distance between a mother's goals for herself and her children and the actual attainment of those goals causes stress. Combine the added ingredients of one, two, three, seven, ten children—all talking, doing, going, planning, trying, and practicing their free agency—then place mother in the center of it all, and it is no wonder mother may feel overpowered at times, perhaps even trapped. To keep sane, each mother needs a solid defense against mother abuse.

The first secret in combatting mother abuse lies in knowing that each child is passing through natural cycles, and that each stage has many growing pains. Mother can avoid getting uptight if she doesn't go through roller-coaster dips and rises with each child each day. When she hears contention in another room, finds an unmade bed, or signs a poor report card, she can say to herself: "I am imperfect too. I was not perfect as a child. This child is in a cycle. He will someday be married, raising his own children, teaching them much like I am teaching him now. I will not give up. I will continue to love him, smile at him, discipline him, and endure this moment, because in a few years both he and I will be grateful."

As mothers, we try to practice techniques that will build our children's self-image. We try not to label them or call them names. We try to listen and read not only what is said but what is not said. We have learned not to compare them to anyone else, and that we are their mirrors. We try to use constructive criticism and proper praise. However, balancing a child's needs and our own needs is a real trick that most of us are not fully equipped to handle.

Power Struggles

But there are several secret defenses mother can use to keep both her own and her child's self-esteem healthy. Take power struggles for example. Power struggles are mini-battles between children and parents. Power struggles often result in win/lose or lose/lose relationships. Power struggles create winners and losers. Let's look at a typical morning for many of us. Mother insists that Tom make his bed before leaving for school. Tom leaves without making it. Score: Tom 1, Mother 0. The next day Mother stops Tom as he is about to leave again without making his bed. Mother takes Tom by the arm and watches over him as he sloppily makes his bed. Score: Tom 0, Mother 0. The next day Mother again stops Tom as he is sneaking out. She tells him if he doesn't make his bed perfectly, right now, she will get out the ping-pong paddle. Tom makes his bed fairly neatly. Score: Tom 0, Mother 1. The best way to handle these situations is to make as many of them win/win as possible.

About a month ago I announced in a family council that it was a mother's right to live in a clean and tidy house. Everyone agreed. Next I told them if they were too busy or too tired to clean their rooms each morning that it was fine with me. There was suspicious silence. I continued to explain that since I have the right to live in a clean and tidy house, and since they do not have to keep their rooms clean, I had employed a maid to clean up after any child who did not take time to clean his room. There were cheers. The maid's services would begin every morning as soon as the children had gone to school. Then I mentioned that the maid did not come free. I said that we were lucky and got a very reasonable maid who only charged one dollar per room for any two days in a week. If the room was left undone more than two days a week, the price of the maid went up to five dollars per room per day. There was interested silence. I then produced a jar with a label on it that read "For the Maid." Then I bowed and said, "Meet the maid."

The next morning every bed but one was made. I quickly ran downstairs and made that child's bed and put away a few clothes and books. Then I wrote a note, "Mike owes the maid $1.00," and dropped the note in the jar. It didn't take long for the word to pass that I really meant business. In the past month I, the maid, have earned only four dollars. Business in that respect has not been very good, but I have enjoyed four clean bedrooms every morning. This has been an excellent way to avoid power struggles. I've even had three children who have offered to be the maid.

One way to make power struggles win/win was explained to me by a friend. She told me about some difficulty she was having with her fourteen-year-old son. He seemed to be unhappy at home and she was his number one target while he vented his frustrations. My friend said that she made this problem a matter of prayer. One day an idea came to her. Every time this boy came to her for anything, or the first time she saw him in the morning, or when he came home from school, the first thing she did was smile at him.

She said that after a few weeks of greeting her son with a smile whenever she saw him, she saw no improvement in him. But she did feel a difference within herself. She felt the tension and annoyance lessen. Soon she found that she could pat him on the back or put her arm around his shoulder without him rebuffing her. Today, two years later, their relationship is stronger. Not all his problems are solved, but he knows he has a loving and supportive mother. This undeclared war was reduced to occasional minor skirmishes.

When my friend told me this, I was reminded of the chapter in *Your Child's Self-Esteem*, by Dorothy Briggs, that tells mothers that they are their children's mirror. When a child looks at his mother, he can tell by the expression on her face and by the attention she gives him how much she esteems him.

This story also reminded me of an English class I taught. It contained thirty-two eighth graders—twenty-four of them were boys. This particular class had just about driven me to an early retirement. The twenty-four boys came to English right after Boys' Chorus. They were always hyped up and not interested in English. One day I found out how they felt I valued them.

It was the final report-card day of the year. I was busy interviewing each student, one at a time, at my desk. I showed the students what grade they had earned and counseled them on how to be better students. Suddenly, the most troublesome boy called out, "Hey, Mrs. Linford." I looked up at him with a how-dare-you-interrupt-me-again look. Flash went his camera. All the students laughed. "We just wanted to get your picture with that look on your face that we've seen all year," he said.

From that embarrassing incident I should have learned what a powerful form of silent communication the smile can be. You don't have to say anything, it shows in your face. The smile is a major defense in the strategy against lose/lose or win/lose power struggles.

One other good way to avoid power struggles is to give lots of genuine, specific praise. A sincere compliment softens and heals as nothing else can. Even if criticism is necessary, it can be swallowed if it is sandwiched between two slices of genuine praise.

Negotiation

Even if mother does everything right—reflects in her face that she esteems her child, reinforces positive behavior with praise, avoids power struggles, and creates win/win solutions—she also needs negotiating skills to combat potential mother abuse. Here are a few tips I've learned about negotiating with children:

Situation: The child asks for permission to do something or go somewhere.

1. Do a little investigative work before answering. Find out when, where, who with, who is driving, whose money, what movie, and whatever else. Then make a decision based on fact.

2. Only say no if you are willing to stand firm no matter how much pleading, crying, or verbal or psychological abuse you have to endure.

3. Only say yes if you won't later change your mind or complain about the consequences.

Situation: You need a child to do something.

1. Ask as though you expect a positive response.

2. If you get any of the standard "no" responses, like "I don't have time," or "You always ask me," try negotiating with a smile or an arm around the shoulder saying, "I really appreciate your help."

3. If that doesn't work, you have two choices. You could give the child a break: "I know how busy you are, and you don't have to do it right now. What time would you be able to do it?" In this way the child makes an agreement, a verbal contract. You could also use your superior size and strength and insist the child respond now. "I am the mother. You will do what I say when I say it." Good luck if you choose the latter, because you might only have superior size and strength for a few years.

4. When the task is done remember to express your thanks.

Situation: A child asks for permission to do something

or go somewhere in the future, but has no definite plans. "Hey, Mom, what would you say if next summer, after I get my driver's license, we drive to Mexico?"

1. Don't commit yourself to anything more than a week away. (This is said a bit tongue in check. Of course there are long-range plans that must be made well in advance.)

2. Don't commit yourself to plans that later could be embellished by the child.

3. Say something like, "That sounds like a lot of fun. Ask me again when it's closer to the time and you have definite plans."

Situation: A child asks for permission to do something, your decision is no, and the child vigorously protests. (This creates an opportune moment for a win/win agreement.)

1. In the beginning don't respond with an emphatic no. Soften the no with a phrase like, "It does sound like it could be a lot of fun, but I feel that because of these reasons I am going to say no." Then list the reasons.

2. Then ask the child if he has thought of changing the plans to eliminate the problems. Let the child learn to think in alternatives.

3. If you have no concrete reasons, you might simply say: "I'm sorry I have to say no, and I really don't have a reason. I am just saying no. I'm grateful for your support and understanding."

Some mothers never say no. It is just too much trouble to stick by a no. When this happens, the child is in the driver's seat, and even more important, the mother and child never develop any negotiating skills. The power struggle continues in a lose/lose standoff. Even though the child gets his way, he is not truly happy. He becomes more and more demanding and less and less satisfied with his relationship with his mother.

It is possible to negotiate and have both sides get exactly what they want. Too often we think of compromise rather than negotiation. Compromise means both sides give in a little to meet in the middle. Compromise is good, but often negotiation is better. For example, let's look at two sisters who wanted the same orange. They fought and quarreled. Finally they compromised and cut the orange in half. One sister ate the fruit and threw away the peel. The other sister grated the peel for the cake she was making and threw away the fruit. If they had negotiated, they both could have had twice as much.

Some mothers don't really negotiate. They just say no. Saying no is important at the right time, but some are inclined to say no too often. Children don't need to do everything they want to do or have everything they think they need, but too many no's give the child too many discouraging, deflating experiences. My goal is to say four positive comments to every one criticism, suggestion, or no. Try keeping track for one day and see how many negative and positive things you say. The first time I kept track, I was shocked when my ratio was about one to one. Sometimes a child who is told no too often stops asking for permission. He simply does what he wants to do and takes the consequences—a lose/lose situation for sure.

In negotiating, sometimes one or both parties take extreme positions because they feel they'll get more of what they actually want in the end by overstating their position in the beginning. Then when they give in, they are giving up territory that wasn't wanted anyway. I would caution against this with children. We are not negotiating the price of a used car. We are establishing an up-front, honest relationship of mutual trust that will grow stronger with each passing year. This cannot happen if the child feels he is being manipulated or treated dishonestly.

One Thanksgiving, we made place cards for all the guests coming to to dinner. Each card read "We are thankful for _____ (an adjective) _____ (the guest's name)." Some read, "We are thankful for hard-working Dad." "We are thankful for fun-loving Grandpa." "We are thankful for enthusiastic Anne." Finally we had the right adjective for everyone except me. I couldn't think of a descriptive enough word. Then one of the children suggested the word *constant*. At first I was slightly offended. "We are thankful for constant Mom" was not what I expected. But the more I looked at that place card, the more I felt complimented. Did the children feel I was there when they needed me? Could they anticipate my responses? Did this say that they could depend on me to be consistent and fair? I hope so.

The state of negotiation in your home depends largely on your reputation with your children. Are you predictable? Do you have good problem-solving techniques? Are your responses consistent? Do you strive for win/win situations? So often mother is the judge, jury, and the executioner. Her reputation as a fair negotiator makes her life, as well as her children's lives, more often than not win/win.

Humor

Pages of illustrations could show the benefits of humor in smoothing over tense situations. Humor can eliminate immediate and potential problems and lift the entire family's morale. Nothing else can substitute for the ability to see the bright side, the silver lining, the pun, the fun, or the innocent mischief. One way I have found to allow humor to be more of a part of my life is to wait a few seconds between an incident and my response. I find if I react to a situation immediately, without any lag time, my response is often negative. But if I wait even a few seconds, I am more likely to see a bright side.

I remember the day my three oldest children painted themselves with mud because they wished that they had been born Indians. I remember the day I walked in to the boys' bedroom to find that their drawers and closet had been emptied out all over the floor because they were playing sailing and needed an ocean. Clothes were the best ocean they could think of. I reacted to these different situations in two ways. I'll give myself an *A* on the first reaction, but an *F* on the second.

In the mud episode, I ran to get the camera to take their picture. That picture has helped us remember one of our family's favorite stories. But on the other occasion, when I saw the mess their ocean voyage had made, I told them to pick up and fold every item of clothing before lunch, without any help from me. Because I reacted quickly, without taking time to think, the fun of that ocean adventure was missed.

I am grateful that my oldest son has the gift of humor. I have learned many things from him. One afternoon I was hanging wallpaper in the front room. The furniture was all displaced, wallpaper scraps and tools were here and there, and I was wearing an old pair of painted jeans. Toys and leftover lunch were everywhere. In the midst of the mess, Matt, then eighteen, came home with a new friend. He came in, quickly assessed the situation, and with pride said, "Bruce, I'd like you to meet my mother, the inferior decorator."

Humor acts as an emergency escape valve to let off steam and pressure. Humor can reduce stress and tension by diverting attention to something else.

Imperturbability

Being imperturbable means being calm and serene, even in times of stress. It means having a reasonable degree of self-control so that the mother abuse, mild or severe, runs off your back like water off a duck's back. No human can be totally imperturbable. But the more calm, cool, and collected a mother is in daily experiences, the healthier her self-esteem will be.

Sometimes I get tired of being imperturbable. I guess it could be argued that if one tires of being imperturbable that it is not true imperturbability. Perhaps so, but when things begin to bother me, I use the following tricks:

1. I give myself a pat on the back. For example, when

I have worked all day to prepare a special meal that is consumed in twenty minutes and the children begin to ask to be excused, I say, "Thanks Mom for the delicious meal. I know it took all day to prepare it. Julia Child could not have done better." They all laugh and offer their apologies and belated compliments. But the air is already cleared in my mind.

2. I say, "Hey guys, mother abuse is against the law. Be kind to me."

3. I take a magazine and make a long stop in the bathroom.

Acting calm and serene is actually the very best defense against mother abuse. It also prevents more of the same in the future because many little things that could cause power struggles go by without being mentioned. Imperturbability means mother may have to tune out a dripping faucet, piano practices at five o'clock in the morning, rock music, or contention. One of mother's best defenses is to be fairly resilient and basically optimistic.

These four weapons—avoiding power struggles, improving negotiating skills, increasing the use of humor, and becoming more imperturbable—will help combat mother abuse. Stronger relationships with each child and a healthier self-esteem for mother will be the result. We can't expect that mother abuse will be totally eliminated, but it will be diminished if we give and take, and remember that the current cycles will not last forever.

FOUR

Self-Esteem Is a
Self-fulfilling Prophecy

Proverbs 23:7 states, "For as he thinketh in his heart, so is he." In other words, you are what you think. You can be no better than the image you have of yourself in your mind. Self-esteem is a self-fulfilling prophecy.

If your self-esteem is low, this does not mean you have low intelligence, that you lack talent, or that you are not of great value to your family and society. It simply means you do not feel good enough about yourself. If you fall into this category, please do something about it now because low self-esteem is contagious. You can give it to your friends. People with low self-esteem tend to find each other and feed on each other's negative attitudes. Low self-esteem can also be inherited. You can give it to your children. You may have inherited some of it from your parents. Don't pass it on to another generation. Don't inflict your children with the same handicap you have.

I know a father with low self-esteem. He thinks that everyone is out to get him. Every new car he buys is a lemon. Every repairman who comes to his home is incompetent and a cheat. Every social function he is invited to turns sour for him in the first thirty minutes. He is becoming a wrinkled, disagreeable recluse when he should be in his prime. How could this negative view of life not affect his children?

Can you build your own self-esteem? Yes! It will not necessarily be easy, but every notch up the self-esteem ladder means a healthier, happier you. You may not believe that happier and healthier go together. Many recent studies, however, indicate that often happier and healthier walk hand in hand.

One of the clearest statements of this, involving a study done at Johns Hopkins University, was reported in the October 1981 *Reader's Digest*. An article entitled "How Emotions Rule our Health" gives evidence that when we are emotionally upset, we trigger a chain of events that involve the brain and the endocrine system. Severe overstimulation of neuroendocrine response may have physical effects that lead to disease. The article reports studies that have shown that the immune system may be lowered during times of stress and that defenses against infections and tumors are therefore diminished. Also, increased heart rate, elevated blood pressure, and higher levels of free fatty acids in the blood have been reported. If these conditions are prolonged, migraines, hypertension, and even coronary heart disease or stroke may result. Dr. Caroline Bedell Thomas, head of the Johns Hopkins study, reports that "anybody who does not believe that emotions and disease are linked is ill-informed."

So building your self-esteem may well affect your physical health. But, just how does a woman go about building her own self-image? First, do a little inventory.

The following questions will provide a guide to help you measure how healthy your self-esteem is. Answer yes or no to each question:

1. I like doing things by myself.
2. I enjoy thinking through problems and making my own decisions.
3. I can admit mistakes and defeats without feeling inferior.
4. I can take a difference of opinion without feeling put down.
5. I can accept a gift or a compliment with a simple

"thank you." I do not feel that I have to give a compliment back or tell why I don't deserve the compliment.

6. I can laugh at myself on occasion without feeling overly embarrassed.
7. I feel free to express my feelings even when they differ from my peers.
8. I can be alone without feeling lonely.
9. I can let others be right or wrong without feeling that I have to correct them.
10. I can appreciate and enjoy the accomplishments of others almost as much as my own.
11. I can tell a story about myself without bragging.
12. I go around trying to please other people much of the time.
13. I welcome new challenges with confidence.
14. I don't blame others for my mistakes. I can say "I'm sorry."
15. I can fail and still be willing to try again.
16. I make friends easily.
17. I trust most other people.
18. I usually expect things to turn out as I plan.

Give yourself a point for every yes answer, unless you answered yes to number twelve. Number twelve should be a no answer. (If you go around trying to please other people all the time, you do so at the expense of your own self-esteem.) If you got less than twelve points, you will definitely benefit, as I did, from the following steps that will help you build your self-esteem. Even if you got all eighteen points possible, you may learn some things you didn't know.

Step one: Put the past behind you by writing a "blame" list. "I am the way I am because Aunt Minnie slapped me when I was ten." Or, "I was the eleventh child in my family and my father worked in a bar playing the guitar." Or, "I didn't make pep club in high school and that caused me to . . ." Or, "My father always . . ." Or, "My mother never . . ." Make the list complete. This is a onetime deal. You can only make a blame list once, so put everything that you can blame on someone else on the list. Make sure you include physical traits you don't like and blame them on some relative. "I got my big nose from Grandpa Nelson." "My tendency to gain weight must have come from Grandma Brown."

When the list is finished, look it over to make sure it is complete. Then have a little ceremony to destroy this list. Incinerate it, tear it in a million pieces, or flush it away. Let the destruction of the list be symbolic of erasing your negative feelings about your past. The past is passed. Nothing can change the events, but your attitude about the past can change.

The choice you have is either to waste your life being negative and assessing blame and consequently being less effective now because of what happened then, or to go forward putting the negative past in the past and make the most of now.

Step two: Have confidence in God. Our Father in Heaven wants you to think highly of yourself. He wants you to be successful. You are his child, with a divine mission. He can help you build your self-esteem. Confidence in God is called faith. Faith is often misunderstood. Faith is not hope. Hope precedes faith. Hope is the wishing, the planning, the thinking. Faith is the action, the work, the try and try again that makes something a reality.

If you ask your Heavenly Father for help in building your worn-out confidence, he can bring ideas to your mind, open doorways, provide opportunities, and change attitudes—whatever you need. Ask for his help. Show your faith in him by working to make the things you pray about come to be. Listen for his still, small voice and act on his promptings.

Step three: Have faith in yourself. In raising children's self-esteem, one of the most important rules is to show them that you have faith in them. You show them that you trust them. You treat them as though you know they will make good decisions. You must do the same for yourself. Have faith in yourself. Since faith is a principle of action, act by setting a goal to overcome your low self-esteem; then go to work. You do not have faith in something or someone unless your works show it.

Often women show their low self-esteem with comments such as "I'm ready for another disappointment," "I gave up," "The competition was too much for me," "I tried out for two choirs but neither one wanted me," or "I've always been so clumsy." This method of advertising your low self-esteem brings believers to your side. If you treat yourself as unsuccessful, others will treat you as though you are unsuccessful, and you will feel unsuccessful. The more you repeat your failures or unsuccessful moments, the more these negative labels you place on yourself become a stumbling block to your self-esteem.

If you constantly call a child stupid, he will believe you. If you constantly demean yourself, you will not only convince yourself of your inadequacies, but others will believe you as well. This kind of name-calling and labeling that reinforces your own low self-esteem needs to be eliminated from each personality. Don't be your own worst enemy. Don't continually take the witness stand against yourself. Have enough faith in yourself to keep your lack of self-confidence to yourself.

Women sometimes reveal their low self-esteem in the opposite way. They overcompensate for it by putting up a false front. They mask their inner insecurity with boasting and name dropping. Some women may have nervous mannerisms, such as a loud voice or extra dramatic hand gestures, that call undo attention to themselves. Watch for these two manifestations of low self-esteem in yourself. Try to discipline yourself to break these habits.

Step four: Treat others with respect and dignity. Give salespeople a smile, your patience, and your appreciation. Let the people who deliver your mail, the milk, and the newspaper know that you appreciate them. Treat neighbors as you would like to be treated. Pay respect and you get respect. Show appreciation and you will be appreciated—nowhere is this more important than in your home.

I have often held the upper hand in dealing with our children. I sometimes act like a strict Victorian parent, exacting precise obedience and service. But every time I fall into this trap, I find I have created a distance between my children and me. Because of this, I started an experiment a few years ago. I began to give genuine service to my children, not when they demanded it but when they deserved it.

When my seventeen-year-old was rushed with many pressures and obligations, I took advantage of the opportunity and ironed a blouse for her. I taught one of her piano students. I had a favorite meal ready for her. I plugged in the curling iron without her having to ask me. I said thoughtful, comforting words. The results were amazing. In the next few days, she treated me like a queen. She kept repeating over and over how much I had done for her, and how much she appreciated it. She helped me curl my hair. She offered to let me wear her new sweater, and the pressure she had been under seemed lighter. (If she had demanded service, however, that would not have been the time to give it. A selfish, demanding child needs a mother who calmly says, "I'm sorry you are so rushed," and then quietly goes about her own business. This builds the child's self-esteem and the mother's.)

Self-respect grows as you show respect. If you do not gossip or find fault with others, you will be less inclined to find fault with yourself. You will not only gain respect for yourself, but others will respect you more as well.

Step five: Watch for your successes and praise yourself. In helping children develop a high self-esteem, we make sure they have many success experiences. We have them take ballet, piano, flute, or art lessons. We arrange for them to be on soccer teams. We let them have friends

over and help them with their homework. We hug them
and tell them we love them. We praise them for their successes and encourage them when they *almost* succeed.
Praising is a key to a child's healthy self-image.

One of our daughters recently ran for a student-body
office in her junior high. She did not win, but winning or
losing has little to do with praising. She had worked hard
on her campaign. She had a clever slogan. Her posters
looked professional. I was very proud of the way she accepted the results. I am proud of the way she has carried
on. I told her these things. I could have said, "Well, if
only you had—" I could have added to her feelings of defeat. But she was successful. Praise builds, criticism des-
troys.

We can help children grow up to have skills that they
can feel good about, if we will praise them for their efforts. A healthy self-esteem must have a firm foundation
of real success experiences.

You must have experiences with success also. The
hard part is that you must arrange your own successes
and then praise or compliment yourself. Begin now to
feel good about the things you do. You don't have to win
the blue ribbon at the fair to feel good about the pie you
just baked. You don't have to be mother of the year to
feel good about the way you worked out that last problem. Don't compare yourself to anyone. Be grateful for
each little success. Begin to build a repertoire of success
experiences, and give yourself praise for a job well-done.

You don't have to be an active participant to feel success either. Learn to appreciate music, dance, art, or literature. Be successful at enjoying. You don't have to be a
great athlete to feel pride or success in sports. Root for a
favorite team. Share in their success. You don't have to
win to feel that you have played well.

You can also enjoy many mini-successes: have the
kitchen presentable on Tuesday before ten o'clock in the
morning, don't raise your voice before eleven, have a
"real" dinner on Friday, exercise for five minutes, or

read one verse of scripture. Lay a foundation for your self-esteem to build on. Then compliment yourself. Don't compare your little success to what you perceive as another's big success. Be proud of your accomplishments no matter how small, and give yourself a pat on the back. In other words, be your own best friend.

Step six: Never give up. Don't be discouraged if your progress is not as dramatic as you had hoped for. These mini-successes are the building blocks of large successes. Maybe today you set a goal to get ten shirts ironed. Even if you only get one finished, that's enough to get your husband to work tomorrow. You can feel good about that. Maybe your goal is to praise yourself if you don't ever yell at anyone. But even if you make it through only one difficult situation without yelling, that's still progress. You can feel good about that. Maybe you want to balance your bank statement. You may not be able to, but you can feel good about trying.

Your Father in Heaven is ready to help you keep trying. He has said: "If men [and women] come unto me I will show unto them their weakness. I give unto men weakness that they may be humble; and my grace is sufficient for all men that humble themselves before me; for if they humble themselves before me, and have faith in me, then will I make weak things become strong unto them." (Ether 12:27.) With Heavenly Father's help, your weaknesses will turn to strengths, and you will be able to defeat discouragement.

Now that you've finished this chapter, I want you to take an inventory of yourself; it's really an inventory of possibilities. I want you to ask yourself these questions: "What would I do if I knew success was assured? What would I do if I knew that I could not fail? Where would I go? What would I have? What would I become?" Answer these questions and see if you can get an idea of the kind of success you could have if you begin to have faith in yourself today—good luck!

FIVE

Your Husband
Can Affect Your Self-Esteem

Some days, when everything has gone wrong, you look at the clock and see that there are only fifteen minutes before hubby is due home. You push your fast-forward button and in fourteen minutes the house is tidied, the table is set, the dinner is ready, the children's faces are washed, and a splash of blush is on your cheeks. You forget the discouraging moments of the day and optimistically plan for a positive evening with your husband.

This sets the stage for several possible endings. Your husband can come home and put his arms around you and say, "I love you. It's great to be home." Better yet, he can come in and say, "I love you. It's great to be home. What can I do to help?" Or he can come in, look around, and say, "Last-minute rush, huh? What did you do all day? If you could just get organized like I am at the office, you'd sure get a lot more done. Is that Mexican food I smell again?"

Your husband is entitled to come home after a frustrating day at the office and receive all the tender loving care you can muster. But if your husband expects when his eight-hour day is over that the rest of the time is for his relaxation and pleasure, you should somehow make him aware that *you* are never off duty. Whoever said that a "mother's work is never done" spoke the truth.

Husbands who realize the constant responsibility that

weighs on a wife and mother, especially a wife who also works outside the home, can lift much of that burden with a few sincere words of appreciation and some significant help.

The husband contributes greatly to the level of esteem his wife has for herself. He also determines to a large degree how the children treat their mother. I saw a plaque recently that read: "The most important thing a father can do for his children is love their mother." Father is the one who sets the pattern in the home for the way his wife is treated by their children. If he rebuffs her by an unkind or sarcastic remark, or if he belittles, scolds, or finds fault with her, the children will treat her likewise.

If instead, father treats his wife with affection, acknowledges her efforts, and firmly insists that the children treat her with respect; if his actions set an example of patience, gentleness, and understanding; if he protects his wife from the mother abuse he witnesses, he contributes as no other person can to her happiness and self-esteem.

How blessed a wife and mother is to have a husband who comforts her, who is a loyal friend, and who is part of the solution rather than part of the problem. Then husband and wife, father and mother, are partners who are unified in facing the world together.

Although few of us have absolutely ideal circumstances, there are some women who find themselves living with verbal or psychological abuse from their husbands. If a woman finds herself in this kind of a situation, what can she do? Every case is different, but I believe she has five basic choices:

1. She can realize that people who abuse others have a low self-esteem. She can, therefore, try to build her husband's self-esteem so that he will, as a consequence of feeling better about himself, treat her better.

2. She can bear the abuse and get on with life the best she can.

3. She can give her husband an ultimatum: either he can treat her kindly or get out.

4. She can try to educate her husband as to her needs, and then they can work together to improve each other's self-esteem.

5. She can get professional help.

I do not presume to have all the answers for women who find themselves in unpleasant situations. However, I would like to share with you the experiences of some friends of mine and how they handled the problems presented to them.

I have a friend whose husband is well-respected in the community. They have all that money can buy. He is a good father. Her problem was that he used to abuse her—not physically, but intellectually. He has two university degrees. She spent one year at a university and then quit when they were married so that she could support him in school. He used to constantly demean her lack of education by making comments such as: "She never reads the newspaper," "Don't ask her. She didn't even get through liberal education classes," and "Our children got their brains from their father." After making these statements, he would laugh heartily, as though they were good jokes.

I asked her, "Have you ever told him how you feel?" She said that she hadn't told him because she felt that most of his comments were basically true. "The only thing that is true," I boldly said, "is that your husband is ungrateful for the wonderful wife he has and is extremely rude." She decided to explain her feelings to him.

When she spoke to him, she used "I feel" messages. She said, "I feel hurt when you make a joke about my limited education. I would have loved to finish school. I want to be your intellectual equal, and I hope to get a university degree." He was surprised that she felt hurt. He realized that she had sacrificed for him, and he now tries to make only positive comments.

Tell your husband what he does that makes you feel helpless, trapped, or unloved. Don't accuse him with "you" messages: "You are the cause of all my frustrations." Instead send "I feel" messages. As you show genuine concern for your husband, as you help to build his self-esteem, he will usually reciprocate. An open, honest relationship will win with time. Teamwork and open communication will contribute to a good marriage and will build self-esteem in both partners.

My sister told me a story of her friend who had an intolerable marriage. She went to an attorney and said, "I not only want a divorce, but I want it to hurt my husband as much as it can for as long as it can. I want to know that he will suffer for all the suffering he has caused me."

The attorney said that he knew a good way to make her husband suffer. He instructed this woman to go home and, for the next six months, to be the most ideal wife possible. He told her to cook her husband's favorite meals, have the home clean and happy, help him succeed in his work, support him in his hobbies, and compliment him. Then after six months of being the perfect wife, she should file for a divorce. "After living with you for six perfect months," the attorney said, "he will feel guilt and remorse the rest of his life."

This woman thought this was a good idea and went home and did as she was instructed. A couple of years later she met the attorney in the mall.

"Don't we have some unfinished business?" he asked.

"No," she said with a smile. "No, we don't." It seemed that her husband changed so much when she changed that a divorce was no longer necessary.

As is pointed out by this story, I believe that any woman would benefit from checking her attitude from time to time. How we choose to react to our husbands can make all the difference in the quality of our relationships. If there was one-half glass of rootbeer on the counter, would you say, "How come I only get half a glass of rootbeer?" Or would you say, "Wow! I get half a glass of rootbeer. Thanks!" Your positive attitude can make even the most difficult times better.

The last example I would like to share with you is from the life of a friend of mine whose husband became interested in another woman. (Could there be anything more damaging to a wife's self-esteem?) She wept through the entanglement that brought them to the brink of divorce. She sought advice. Nearly everyone who advised her said, "Throw the guy out. He's no good." Well, she couldn't throw him out; she loved him. So she endured, and she prayed. He moved out and broke covenants. Her self-esteem was terribly damaged. But, in this case, patience won. Today, they are still married. He has repented. He is sorry. He can't imagine how he allowed himself to be trapped by immorality. He feels guilty that his wife and children suffered because of him. How thankful he is that he has a wife who spent a year of her life worrying, crying, and praying over him, a wife who never gave up. He shudders to think that she could have left him, as many who find themselves in similar circumstances do.

If you ever get to the point that you think divorce is the only solution, remember that statistics show that first marriages are much more likely to succeed than second marriages. Unless extreme conditions exist, the best prospect might be to keep working through your problems together.

My husband, Richard, and I have hit on a method of sorting out our feelings that cause friction. About once a week, usually on a Sunday evening, we give each other an interview. My questions to him include these: How is your work going? Do you feel good about your boss? Do you feel successful in your work? Do you enjoy your Church calling? Do you feel that I am supportive? What are your goals for this week? Do you obey the speed limit? How are you getting along with each of our children? How do you feel about being a father? How is your relationship with your wife? Are you happy in your marriage? What is the one thing you hope your wife is working on changing? Is there something you need me to do this week?

His questions to me are much the same. He always includes these three: Are you remembering your prayers? Do you read your scriptures daily? Do you love your husband in spite of all his faults?

My answers to these questions are always the same. "I try." "No." "You bet!"

Be optimistic. Expect things to go your way even though it is not always easy. Have hope and faith that things will generally go well. Realize that while a happy marriage will help your self-esteem, your husband is not in charge of your self-esteem. He is in charge of his own self-esteem. *You* are in charge of yours.

SIX

Your Emotional Self-Esteem

We often joke about being depressed or about how our children drive us crazy, but we know we really aren't mentally ill—at least, we hope not. This book is not meant to be enough help for the severely depressed or the mentally ill, for whom professional help is necessary. When I use the words *depression* and *mental health,* I do not use them in the clinical sense. These terms are used to describe the frustrations, discouragements, and weariness that are part of life.

The line between this part-of-life depression and true, clinical depression is when a woman cannot bounce back on her own. If helplessness turns into a way of life, if feelings of being out of control become chronic, if the desire to be resilient is gone, it is time to get professional help.

Some depressions are merely worn spots in the shag carpet, some are chuckholes, and some are mile-long valleys. Some depressions and related problems are too deep to climb up and out of alone.

Here are some questions you could ask yourself to help you decide if you should consider professional counseling:

1. Is this problem disrupting normal processes such as eating and sleeping?
2. Do you have wide mood swings: elated one minute and deeply depressed the next?

3. Is your anxiety or depression becoming chronic?
4. Do you feel alienated from others?
5. Do you feel apathy, guilt, remorse, or anguish?
6. Do you feel physically or psychologically numb?
7. Are you disinterested in life?
8. Do you feel unable to experience pleasure?
9. Do you have suicidal thoughts?
10. Have you had a sudden weight loss or gain?
11. Do you feel that no one cares, that no one understands, that no one can help, or that your life has little value?

If you answered yes to any of these questions, discuss your concerns with a trusted friend: your husband, parent, visiting teacher, or your Father in Heaven. If this does not quiet your apprehensions and no solution seems forthcoming, contact your doctor or your bishop for advice. Whatever you do, don't try to treat your depression with drugs prescribed for someone else.

A woman I know was feeling depressed one day, and her friend said to her, "If I bring over a valium, will you take it?" Don't take even one mood-altering drug unless it is prescribed for *you* by a competent doctor who knows your complete history. And even then, be careful. In the last year, two of my friends have been in the hospital for drug dependency. These women were not addicts in the illegal sense, but they were addicts just the same. They were both desperately dependent on prescription drugs. If your depression seems to be in the mile-long-valley category, take the appropriate action to get help.

Preserving Mental Health

One Sunday morning about seven years ago, I arrived at church on time. That's a feat any mother can be proud of, especially when the opening song is sung at eight-thirty. I was feeling quite good about the way the morning had gone. Our whole family was there on time. The house was fairly tidy, and the crock pot was cooking dinner.

I was nearly to the Relief Society room when a friend stopped me. "You look like you need mental-health time," she said looking at me with pity. I had thought I looked rather nice. "What's mental-health time, and what do I look like?" I asked. She said I appeared haggard and depressed. "Whenever I feel everyday problems are winning the race," she said, "I declare a personal holiday and take time off from the routine. You aren't any good to anyone if you aren't feeling on top of things." (This friend is a nurse who works full time. In spite of her schedule, she calendars mental-health evenings, or Saturdays, when she needs them.)

Mental-health time is a day, half day, or hour—if that's all you can get—that you use to get your mental, emotional, physical, spiritual, and intellectual self back in sync. You use this time any way you choose as long as it helps. It may be a time to evaluate on paper where you are, where you are going, and how you are going to get where you really want to be. It may be a time to write a long overdue letter or to write in your journal. It may be a day to leave breakfast dishes in the sink and scrub the shower instead. It may be a day for rest and relaxation. Whatever you do, the purpose is to recharge your battery. It is a time to get feeling in charge again. It's a time to say, "Stop world! I refuse to keep running at this pace!"

If it is a nap you need, ask a neighbor to watch the children for a few hours, or take a pillow with you in the car and sleep while you wait for a child at a piano lesson. If you need a little lift, have a mental-health lunch. In my case that is anything besides leftovers, tomato soup, or P&J (peanut butter and jelly) sandwiches. If you need to get out of the house, try going to the mall or working in the garden for an hour. If you feel intellectually dull, find an hour to read something challenging. If you have fifty or so things that absolutely must be done, decide which one is most critical. Do it and give yourself a pat on the back.

If you feel burdened with an unfair share of problems, call a friend with more problems than you. If you feel unloved, surprise a friend or family member with some unsolicited service. Giving service is one of the best ways to relieve depression. If you feel melancholy, if the weather has you down, if you are struggling through a crisis, if the tides of fortune are seemingly against you, if the work load has buried you, if there is no money for that much needed pair of shoes, or if you feel exhausted, declare mental-health time and see if it won't help. Perhaps if you only have five minutes, maybe the best way to spend it is on your knees.

One caution: mental-health times should be reserved, maybe even rationed, to be the most effective. You've probably already realized that you are the most productive and happy when you are the busiest. Keep busy, work hard, but know that when external demands exceed your internal supply, you can take mental-health time. Recently I planned a mental-health day. After only an hour, I felt refreshed enough to return to my daily routine.

There are two other ideas that can help with mental and emotional self-esteem.

I Am in Control

I know that I am in charge of myself. That statement seems obvious, but it includes being in charge of moods and thoughts. Do you ever think someone has hurt your feelings? "Grandma hurt my feelings when she chose to spend the weekend with Dana rather than with us." Do you ever think a negative thought, then say, "I couldn't help it; it just popped into my head?" Do you ever say to the children, "You guys are giving me a headache?" If you do, you are deceiving yourself. You alone are in charge of what thoughts and subsequent emotions come into your mind. Only you can expel a negative thought by exchanging it for a better one.

The brain doesn't accept vacuums. It is impossible to

think of nothing. If you want to get rid of a thought, you must immediately replace it.

If you don't believe you control your thoughts, who does? Try this experiment. Think of an alligator. What color is your alligator? If it is the normal greenish, brownish, swamp color most alligators are, change it to red. Now put a tuxedo on your alligator. Did you do it? Of course you did. You just proved you are in control of your thoughts.

You are also the one who is in control of the emotions that come because of your thoughts. Your children can't give you a headache, but you can. You allow yourself to be stressed to the point that you give yourself a headache. The correct statement is, "I was so irritated by your behavior that I gave myself a headache."

Here is an experiment to see if you control your emotions. Next time you feel your tolerance tank nearing empty and you can feel a you-guys-are-giving-me-a-headache statement coming on, stop for one second to take a mental time-out. Transport your thought and emotion to the oasis in your mind where past peaceful memories are stored. Go there for just a moment. Then quickly come back to reality and see if you aren't better equipped to handle the situation.

This is the point of this chapter and the whole book. If you rely on others to build your self-esteem, you will not have a healthy self-esteem. If you expect others to make you happy, you will be disappointed. Also, if you treat others like they are responsible for your happiness or self-esteem, you place unrealistic burdens on your relationship with them.

After reading this, you may think that I am totally emotionally independent, that I never rely on others for my self-esteem. This is not true. Even though I know that I am solely in charge, at times I still try to blame others for my problems. It is difficult to undo years of thought patterns. Not many of us have been taught to take responsibility for our own thoughts and moods. We

haven't been taught to say, "I distressed myself today," or
"I allowed myself to feel hurt," or "I made myself angry,"
or "I let that negative thought stay in my mind."

Just today a friend called. "I feel depressed. My sister
makes me so mad," she said. Then she explained that she
had been talking to her sister on the phone when suddenly
her sister became angry and hung up on her. Of course,
it is easy to see the problems here. (It always is when it's
someone else's problem.) The sister has the problem, not
my friend. But the point is, my friend did not say, "I have
allowed myself to feel depressed because my sister hung
up on me." She said, "My sister made me mad."

This tendency to think others cause our emotions can
be unlearned with conscious effort and practice. Try to
catch yourself attributing a thought or emotion to someone or something else. Stop yourself short, and then
verbalize how a woman who knows she is in charge of her
thoughts and moods would respond. It is possible to make
progress in both taking the responsibility ourselves and
also in freeing others from expectations they can't meet.

Disappointments

We all know that disappointments are a part of life.
But if you are like me, you actually think they are part of
everyone else's life. When something that happens only
to other people happens to us, we say, "Hey, that wasn't
in the script." Others have car accidents, are diagnosed
with cancer, have a handicapped child, or lose their jobs.
I can be very philosophical about how it rains on the just
and the unjust, but give me a problem, a little personal
rain, and I feel persecuted.

I have learned several ways to help protect myself
from the letdown that comes with disappointments. I'd
like to share them with you.

1. Be realistic. Don't expect to win the marathon if
you can't even run the mile.

2. Think in alternatives. Be flexible. If one door
closes, try the back door or even a window.

3. View a disappointment as something that can teach you. Learn the lesson and move forward.

4. Admit to yourself that you are disappointed, but don't lick your wounds very long.

5. Know that some disappointments are inevitable. No woman is a Queen Midas who turns everything she touches into gold.

6. Don't give up hope. Be willing to try again.

The Possibility of PMS

About one out of every ten readers will be totally frustrated and more confused and depressed by reading all of the above. If you are in this ten percent, you have probably tried to bounce back and found that sometimes you can and sometimes you can't. You may surround yourself with motivational ideas and gimmicks only to be more frustrated when you can't make yourself act like you feel you should. You may revolt inside when someone says, "If you would only read your scriptures, remember your prayers, or serve others, all your problems will disappear."

PMS (Premenstrual Syndrome) is a broad term given to over 150 physical, emotional, and behavioral symptoms that come and go cyclically with the menstrual cycle. Some of the physical symptoms include fatigue, headache, bloating, breast tenderness, lack of coordination, joint pain, nasal congestion, and constipation. Some of the emotional symptoms are depression, hostility, paranoia, panic, intolerance, insecurity, and change in sex drive. Behavioral symptoms may include binge eating, violence, withdrawal, crying episodes, decreased self-esteem, angry rages, critical comments, suicidal thoughts and attempts.

These symptoms don't necessarily mean you have PMS. Many chronic disorders have the same symptoms. The diagnosis of PMS comes when symptoms occur, disappear, and recur in a predictable pattern that coincides with the menstrual cycle. A typical pattern would start with two symptom-free weeks beginning about the third day of the period, which is followed by two weeks of increasing symptoms leading up to the first days of the period each month.

PMS can victimize women of any age from puberty to post-menopause. At one time, women with PMS were given hysterectomies to correct the problem. Doctors discovered too late for these women that PMS is not centered in the reproductive system. It is rather a malfunction in the pituitary gland. PMS is a hormonal imbalance.

If you have mild or moderate PMS, you can control the symptoms with certain life-style changes. If you have severe PMS—your symptoms are debilitating and you feel out of control—you need professional help. Unfortunately, a firm diagnosis of PMS can be reached only after all other physical and mental possibilities have been eliminated. Many women who thought they had PMS have had other diseases or disorders, which were discovered through this process.

The first step in diagnosing PMS is to keep a calendar for three months. Make a graph for each month. Record your temperature each morning before you get out of bed. Then weigh yourself and record it on your chart. Then list any symptoms you experience during the day. If the symptoms do disappear and reappear, take your calendar to your gynecologist for evaluation and referral to a PMS center.

Life does have many ups and downs. Healthy emotional self-esteem, however, helps make traveling life's road more like a journey in a Cadillac than on a Honda scooter.

SEVEN

Your Physical Self-Esteem

About ten years ago when I first thought I was getting old, I saw a cartoon in a newspaper. A middle-aged woman was pointing at herself in the mirror. The caption read: "I don't believe it! You have a child in college!" I clipped it out and saved it. It means a lot to me now that I have a child in college.

The years do bring changes to our physical appearance, our general health, our stamina, and our ability to work. Knowing that the years will change the color of my hair, that my skin will sag and wrinkle, and that someday someone will call me "Grandma," does not change the fact that I don't want to age. But, aging is better than the alternative.

Physical appearance and self-esteem are closely linked. I think that looking in the mirror and basically being happy about the reflection is important. A becoming hairstyle, the right makeup, a reasonably attractive figure, and comfortable clothing contribute to an "I'm OK" feeling.

As I have matured, I have noticed that a beautiful face at age seventy or eighty is not due to beautiful features but rather to the character shining through. Every woman can be beautiful, even classic, in her later years because of her strong character. The older ladies in our neighborhood and family are beautiful because of their years of love and service and right choices. The years pay honor to the quality of life lived. When I am in the temple, I look from face to face and am impressed with the uniqueness and beauty of each person.

Your physical appearance says to others how you esteem yourself. If you have a sloppy appearance, are grossly overweight, have sagging posture or a "dead fish" handshake, or can't look others in the eye, you might as well wear a sign: "I have low self-esteem."

Sensible Eating

"Slim is in, and fat is not where it's at" is the fashion today. However, not everyone has the body build to be as slim as the TV models and still maintain health. Each body and each metabolism is unique; each woman must find her own healthy weight. The super-slim look of the eighties will pass.

Sensible eating excludes fad diets. Those diets that do not include the basic four food groups in correct proportion and those that reinforce bad eating habits do much more harm than good, because they do not provide permanent solutions. Behavior modification plans such as Weight Watchers and the Heart Association diet are excellent to change attitudes toward food. Yet, all the world's methods must come in second place to the divine health code found in D&C 89. Let the Word of Wisdom be your initial guide. You may not need any other.

You can balance your weight where you want it by taking in only as many calories as you can burn. An easy equation to figure how many calories a day you should eat is your ideal weight times fourteen. Say, for example, that I want to weigh 120 pounds. I would multiply 120 pounds times fourteen, which equals 1,680. This is the number of calories I should eat each day to weigh 120 pounds.

So often we eat because we are thirsty or because someone else is eating or because we are stressed, nervous, or tired. I read recently that in many cases the way food is used would classify it as a mood-altering drug. That is a sobering thought.

Most of us will never have the exact figure we would choose if we could. But if we are in control of our eating, that is eating to maintain health rather than for pleasure or because of pressure, if we exercise some and feel fairly fit, then physical self-esteem is a positive factor in overall self-esteem.

Even if you are not as physically fit as you would hope, you can still look good. No matter what your figure, no matter how you would like to look in your clothes, you can still feel good about your appearance if you are well-groomed and dress appropriately.

Recently one of my friends came to church looking especially nice—in fact, beautiful. I told her so. She had chosen a flattering style with colors that complemented her hair and skin tones. She responded, "Well, you know I'd love to be thirty pounds thinner. But I decided no matter what my figure, I still need to look nice. It's amazing what a new dress does for the morale."

Another friend of mine has the habit of weighing herself every morning. If she weighs one pound over her ideal weight, she automatically puts herself on a diet. Very few women can eat anything they want to at any time they choose. (My estimate is only about one percent.) For the majority of us, it takes daily effort to keep the scales pointing at the numbers we are happy about.

Exercise

There are as many ways to exercise as there are people. Going to an aerobics class, to the gym or spa, jogging, walking, playing tennis, or swimming are just a few. With my family responsibilities, going outside my home to get exercise is always short-lived because of the inconvenience. If I have to wake early, drive, change clothes, and shower, I soon give up. Instead, I've tried to make exercise part of daily living. Sometimes I jog on the minitramp while I watch the ten o'clock news. I use the kitchen counter as a ballet barre. I do mock stretch and bend exercises as I load the dishwasher, iron, or vacuum. I try to walk as many places as possible.

We lived in England for three years, and while we were there I had to listen over and over to the lazy-American jokes the English tell. One of the favorite jokes of the women in the ward was the one about the visiting teacher who got in her car and drove across the street to pick up her companion. Then, in order to do their visiting, the two drove back across the street to the house next door to the sister who was driving. I thank my British friends for teaching me the walking habit.

If you can get out of the house to exercise, do it. If you can't, be creative and get your exercise at home.

Protecting Your Precious Health

A neighbor who is crippled with rheumatoid arthritis says, "If you have your health, you have everything." She is especially sensitive to both prevention and health maintenance. Two years ago this neighbor was the stake sports director. Sports were her thing. She was good at all of them. Today, she could not bend down to pick up anything off the floor, even if it was a one-hundred-dollar bill.

She has some interesting suggestions for maintaining health. She emphatically says that each person must be willing to pay what it costs to have qualified physicians diagnose and treat illnesses. Often, she feels, when women's resources are tight, or when they have had an unpleasant or unsuccessful experience with a doctor, they attempt to treat themselves. Knowing when there is the need to see a doctor is critical.

The best way to preserve your health is by eating nutritionally, by exercising, and by seeing a doctor for yearly physical exams, as well as when you are ill. Self-diagnosis and treatment are hazardous to your health.

Each mother has two additional enemies to deal with in keeping a healthy physical self-esteem. They are fatigue and stress.

Fatigue

Fatigue is a level of tiredness that a few uninterrupted nights of sleep won't erase. Fatigue may result from any number of causes: worry, heavy work loads, too little sleep, prolonged pressures, or mental effort that saps energy over extended periods of time.

I learned about severe fatigue after our eighth child was born. He was six weeks premature and had several serious health problems that required round-the-clock attention for months. Even today, four years later, he rarely sleeps through the night. I figure that in the last 1,467 days since his birth, I have had ten nights of uninterrupted sleep. The problem with this is that sleep is more essential to my well-being than food.

When this premature baby was about six weeks old, I knew I was exhausted. I was falling asleep standing up. By the time he was six months old, I knew what fatigue was. I simply felt dull. Even the simple pleasures of life did not bring relief. Then a complication set in. I was desperate for sleep, but the more I needed sleep, the harder it became to sleep. Also the sleep I did get became restless as I awakened several extra times each night without cause. Naps were impossible.

I may never completely win the fatigue battle, but here are a few ideas that help me:

1. When I am so tired that I can't sleep, I don't lie in bed, tossing and turning and stressing myself because I can't sleep. I get up. Yes, I force myself to roll out. Then I put in a load of wash or water the plants or do some other task that needs to be done. Often after I have done some little job, I think, "Oh, I'll just sit here on the couch for a minute, then I'll do something else." Most often I wake up two or three hours later.

2. When I am so tired that I cannot move one muscle and it's the middle of the day, I suggest to the children that we go watch a TV show. I owe a lot to *Sesame Street* for entertaining the children and lulling me to sleep at the same time.

3. Sometimes when sleep is impossible, I lie down on the couch, put an afghan over me, turn on some relaxing music, grab a magazine, and say to myself, "Don't try to sleep. A rest is just as good. Just relax. You might not be able to sleep but you can rest."

4. There are times when a change is as good as a rest. And a rest has to be as good as a nap if that's the best you can do.

5. Sleep sometimes seems to evade me because my brain won't turn off. Problems and consequences always seem bleakest at night. When my mind jumps and skips, racing from one thought to another in fast-forward Technicolor, I say, "I am thinking of nothing. I refuse to think of anything." I keep forcing thoughts out of my mind. I try to see only a blank wall. It often works.

6. Deep breathing exercises sometimes help.

7. Aerobic exercises a few minutes before bedtime has helped me at times.

8. Prayer helps too. In fact, sometimes it has worked so well that I have fallen asleep in the middle of a prayer. I pray I will be forgiven.

Fatigue is an enemy. It saps strength, mental vigor, ability to cope, and the sense of well-being. Every mother needs to establish her own strategy against battle fatigue.

Stress

Stress is fatigue's twin. Stress may cause fatigue, or fatigue may cause stress, or they both could be the symptoms of other problems. Stress is the sick feeling in your stomach that lasts day after day. It's the headache that comes and goes or a migraine that incapacitates. Stress is buckling under seemingly routine conditions. Stress is pressure, strain, tension, disquieting feelings of anxiety, or a burden of weight. Stress is distress that alters equilibrium.

Stress, in physics, is measured in pounds per square inch. Too many pounds per square inch cause the structure to collapse. In people, a similar measurement is not available, but the results are just as real. Whenever a gap exists between expectations and the prospects of achieving, stress occurs.

After I realized that stress was affecting me beyond a normal level, I tried to read all I could about stress. This has convinced me that stress causes more trouble in humans than we are aware of. The books on stress all discuss diseases related to or caused by stress. Hypertension, rheumatoid arthritis, migraine headaches, asthma, and diabetes were but a few of the diseases for which stress was listed as a probable cause. I think every ailment known to man was listed. Stress may cause a disease, increase its severity, or even produce symptoms when the disease does not actually exist. We do not have a measure that will tell us what is being caused by stress and what is not. Often, however, when the causes of the stress are relieved, the symptoms disappear.

A friend told me that she awoke one morning hardly able to move. She spent months suffering intensely from arthritis, and then suddenly all symptoms were gone. About three months later, the symptoms reappeared. After a few years she saw the pattern. When she had a foster child living with them, she had arthritis. When the child left, she recovered. My friend found the solution. She still takes foster children but only for short-term stays. When the cause of the stress can be found, the battle is nearly won.

Limiting Stress

One key in diminishing stress is having the ability to say no. Too often when someone calls to ask me to make a casserole for a family with a new baby, or to attend an extra PTA board meeting, or to sing with a group for a Relief Society lesson, or to go on a field trip with the sixth graders, my immediate response is, "Well, yes, I guess I can." Each yes adds stress if the level of stress is already high.

My rule is this. I only say yes to those things I won't

later complain about. When someone calls to ask if I will do something additional, I first look at my calendar. Then I think to myself, "Will I later complain about doing this?" I figure that I don't get any blessing for those things I do grudgingly anyway. If I agree to help, then I am bound to do so happily.

Sometimes when I have compounded my life and my stress level by saying yes to too many appointments, meetings, and "do good" assignments, I remember the self-esteem test in chapter 4. Being able to say no and knowing that you don't have to please others all the time at the expense of your own needs is a sign of high self-esteem. When a woman tries to please others constantly and gets approval and status by running herself ragged, it may be because she has low self-esteem.

I don't want to be misunderstood. I am a firm believer in helping others and in responding to Church or community assignments, but taking my stress level into consideration is critical. Even sometimes if the bishop calls me to a position, I can say, "Bishop, let me tell you of our situation at this moment. I am eight and one-half months pregnant with triplets. If you feel the Lord still wants me to have this calling, I'll accept. But, if you think I could pass this time, I would be thankful."

I want to say yes for the right reasons. Sometimes there are compelling reasons to sacrifice and say yes, but I also want the wisdom to say no when my health, my husband, my children, or my home will suffer.

Physical self-esteem depends on liking what you see in the mirror and on the scales, on limiting fatigue, on keeping stress under control, and on maintaining your physical health. High physical self-esteem is an important step in achieving an over all healthy self-esteem.

EIGHT

Your Spiritual Self-Esteem

How do you measure your spiritual self-esteem? Is it in the number of Church meetings you attend each Sunday, in the number of charitable acts you do each week, in the number of scriptures you read each day, in the number of prayers you say? Spiritual self-esteem differs from physical self-esteem. You can't just step on a scale to measure gained or lost spiritual depth. You can't run on a treadmill to determine your spiritual prowess.

We all know of individuals who appeared to be spiritually healthy and yet commit serious sin. We know others who never attend a meeting or pay a dime of tithing, but who give daily Christlike service.

Even though there is no quantitative measure, each woman knows when she is spiritually fit. When a woman's spiritual self-esteem is high, she has confidence in her Heavenly Father and in herself as his daughter. The scriptures promise: "Let thy bowels also be full of charity towards all men, and to the household of faith, and let virtue garnish thy thoughts unceasingly; *then shall thy confidence wax strong* in the presence of God; and the doctrine of the priesthood shall distil upon thy soul as the dews from heaven." (D&C 121:45; italics added.)

Spiritual self-esteem is an inner secret that is measured in the mind and heart. I like the scripture found in Luke 2:19; it reads, "But Mary kept all these things, and pondered them in her heart." Isn't that how our spiritual

lives are? Even bearing a testimony does not touch the
true feelings in the heart. Words are inadequate expres-
sions of poignant feelings.

I suppose few of us are as spiritually fit as we would
like to be. I have my spiritual weaknesses. You have
yours. Three aspects of the gospel especially help me to
keep my spiritual self-esteem healthy.

Upon My Holy Day

One of my best sources of spiritual self-esteem has
come from a lesson I learned when our first child was just
a few weeks old. Richard and I went to visit his grand-
mother, Ida Boss. She happily admired yet another great-
grandchild, then turned her attention to me. She took
my hands in hers and spoke seriously. She said, "I am
going to give you my secret for a happy life." As I tried to
think what the secret to her rich and successful life could
be, she said simply, "Keep the Sabbath day holy."

She explained that with eleven children, hustling
around Sunday morning for a lost shoe, or ironing even
one shirt for each child would mean chaos. She told me
that she eliminated this problem by making sure each
Saturday night that every piece of each child's Sunday
clothing was checked for readiness. She told of mixing
extra bread on Saturday for Sunday. She made sure the
entire meal for Sunday was prepared on Saturday. She
had the house "Sunday" clean by Saturday night. All
these preparations meant a more worshipful and peaceful Sabbath. At the time I thought that she really believed
that "Saturday is a special day. It's the day we get ready
for Sunday. We shine our shoes and we go to the store; so
we won't have to work until Monday."

I have tried to follow her counsel. I try to prepare a
Sunday meal on Saturday, but if I don't have time, we
just have something simple that meets the requirement,
"Let thy food be prepared with singleness of heart."
(D&C 59:13.)

I try to have the children's clothes ready on Saturday.

This, however, has become increasingly difficult with
teenage daughters who can never commit on Saturday to
what they are going to wear on Sunday.

We have the house "Sunday" clean on Saturday night
and then just maintain it over Sunday by making beds and
doing dishes. We try to relax, read, have home evening
and interviews with each member of the family. We sing,
sleep, plan the week, talk about what we experienced in
the day's Church meetings, read aloud to each other, write
in our journals, prepare lessons for next Sunday, have
our best conversations, and sometimes play word games.

This advice from Grandma Boss has had impact not
only on our enjoyment of the Sabbath but also on our
readiness for the coming week. I believe the following
blessings promised to those who keep the Sabbath day
holy are literally fulfilled:

"Inasmuch as ye do these things with thanksgiving,
with cheerful hearts and countenances, not with much
laughter, for this is sin, but with a glad heart and a cheerful countenance—verily I say, that inasmuch as ye do this,
the fulness of the earth is yours, the beasts of the field
and the fowls of the air, and that which climbeth upon
the trees and walketh upon the earth; yea, and the herb,
and the good things which come of the earth, whether
for food and for raiment, or for houses, or for barns, or
for orchards, or for gardens, or for vineyards; . . . He
who doeth the works of righteousness shall receive his
reward, even peace in this world, and eternal life in the
world to come." (D&C 59:15-17, 23.)

A Song of the Heart

Hymns ("hers," as our twelve-year-old daughter jokes)
have been, and forever will be, one of my greatest sources
of spiritual strength. Hymns are my spiritual dessert.
When all eight children are divided into camps and a loud
verbal battle is in progress, I think: "Master, the tempest is
raging," and then when it's over, "Peace be still."

At the end of an overwhelming day, I pray: "Abide
with me; 'tis eventide." When I receive bad news, I re-

member: "Fear not, I am with thee, O be not dismayed." When I feel discouraged, I recall: "Count your many blessings; name them one by one, And it will surprise you what the Lord has done." When I am overwhelmed with feelings of deep, humble gratitude, I think: "How wondrous and great thy works, God of praise!"

One evening at the end of a dinner with three other couples, we went to the piano and sang everyone's favorite hymns. A beautiful spirit filled the room and each heart. We sang in harmony: "Come, Come, ye Saints," "I Need Thee Every Hour," "We Thank Thee, O God, for a Prophet," "Praise to the Man," "O My Father," "Sweet Hour of Prayer," "Behold! A Royal Army," and "A Mighty Fortress Is Our God."

Last week I woke up feeling spiritually empty. Worries and fears had settled on me. Wondering how to start the day, I looked around. My eyes rested on the new hymnbook I had just purchased. I sat down and thumbed through it, and toward the end of the book, I saw the words, "Love One Another." I went to the piano and played the hymn. I played it again. Through my tears I could still see the notes well enough to play it a third time. The message was clear and the spirit testified: "As I have loved you, love one another." Sunlight replaced the emptiness of a few minutes before.

I stood up and went over to a bulletin board on which we write notes to each other. I wrote, "As I have loved you, love one another." Within an hour, my visiting teachers, Sue and Judy, knocked at the door. As they entered, Sue handed me a sheet of music—"Love One Another." They then gave me a beautiful lesson about the song. I showed them the words I'd written on the bulletin board, and Judy asked, "How did you know to make us a visual aid?"

Hymns fortify and comfort. How grateful I am for these powerful, sacred words and melodies.

A Prayer unto Me

Prayer—what would we do without it? How can we

calculate its influence? Is there an hour that we don't need our Heavenly Father? The following is Alma 34:19-27 with my own interpretation in brackets.

"Yea, humble yourselves, and continue in prayer unto him. Cry unto him when ye are in your fields [backyard], yea, over all your flocks [belongings]. Cry unto him in your houses, yea, over all your household [your husband and children], both morning, mid-day, and evening. Yea, cry unto him against the power of your enemies. Yea, cry unto him against the devil, who is an enemy to all righteousness. Cry unto him over the crops [appliances] of your fields [houses], that ye my prosper in them. Cry over the flocks [works] of your fields [hands], that they may increase. But this is not all; ye must pour out your soul in your closets [bedrooms], and your secret places [bathrooms], and in your wilderness [on the freeway]. Yea, and when you do not cry unto the Lord, let your hearts be full, drawn out in prayer unto him continually for your welfare, and also for the welfare of those who are around you."

Prayer, the natural inclination of a child to talk to his father, is one of our Heavenly Father's kindest gifts to us.

The Bible dictionary instructs us about prayer: "As soon as we learn the true relationship in which we stand toward God (namely, God is our Father, and we are his children), then at once prayer becomes natural and instinctive on our part." (Matt. 7:7-11.) Many of the so-called difficulties about prayer arise from forgetting this relationship. Prayer is the act by which the will of the Father and the will of the child are brought into correspondence with each other. The object of prayer is not to change the will of God, but to secure for ourselves and for others blessings that God is already willing to grant, but that are made conditional on our asking for them. Blessings require some work or effort on our part before we can obtain them. Prayer is a form of work, and is an appointed means for obtaining the highest of all blessings."

I know that God, my Heavenly Father, knows all things. He knows what is best for me and mine. My responsibility is to pray with faith and then work to make my prayers a reality. I also know that Heavenly Father has many great blessings in store for me. It is my responsibility to ask him for those opportunities, those solutions, those ideas, and those miracles that he desires me to have.

Prayer—what a grand principle and privilege.

NINE

Lessons My
Friends Have Taught Me

For many years, I have had the habit of asking people who had admirable qualities to share with me their ideas, their attitudes, their methods, and even their secrets of success. Through the years, I have gathered many valuable tips. This chapter will introduce you to some of my friends and their ideas that they have shared with me.

Richard: Mission and Priorities

Several years ago my best friend, who also happens to be my husband, suggested a way I could better make decisions based on principle. He had noticed that making choices, taking the right fork in the road, knowing what to do when and which to do first was difficult for me.

He introduced me to the idea of writing a statement of what I thought my mission in life is. After days of thinking, I remembered that Heavenly Father, through his son, had written a mission statement himself (Moses 1:39). I borrowed his words for my own statement:

My Mission in Life

"It is my work and will be my glory to help my Heavenly Father bring to pass my immortality and eternal life and also the immortality and eternal life of my husband, children, and others I may be blessed to influence."

Next, Richard asked me to make a list of the major roles I had in life. I wrote daughter/sister/aunt, mother,

54

wife, Church worker, community worker, friend/neighbor, and extended family member.

He looked over the list and said I'd left off the most important aspect of my life. I reviewed the list and said that I thought it was complete. He reminded me that the person I had total responsibility for, the person whose salvation depended entirely on me, was not on the list. I realized that *I* was not on the list. So I added myself.

Next, he told me to put the list in the order of importance: top priority first. Since I have total responsibility for my own salvation, I must be first on the list. Then I thought my best friend should be next most important, so I listed my role as a wife as number two. Third and fourth were easy: my calling as a mother and my responsibilities as a daughter/sister/aunt.

Then I reasoned that people are always more important than programs and that family was more important than non-family. So next I listed my responsibilities as a member of an extended family and my responsibilities as a friend and neighbor. Then I reasoned that any Church calling would have precedence over community service so I added the contributions I can make by accepting Church callings and then my service to the community.

Now I had a mission statement and had set my priorities. Many decisions were now automatically made. This list, written in my journal, brought an element of order to my life. I now knew where I was going and how to get there.

Joseph Smith: The Law of Particles

Joseph Smith (I hope I can call him a friend) used what he called the Law of Particles as his solution to the constant flow of interruptions he experienced. The Prophet had to endure being interrupted even at the most inconvenient times. He had to greet new Saints and travelers, to counsel members needing advice, to care for his own family, to move or go on missions or respond to the pressures of lawsuits. He had to do all this while carrying on the divine calling of establishing The Church of Jesus Christ of Latter-day Saints.

His solution to being constantly interrupted, and yet needing to accomplish many things, was the Law of Particles. He saw that many large and small duties could be conquered in small bites. His idea is similar to the joke "How do you eat an elephant? A bite at a time." In this way he kept all his projects, all his duties, all his responsibilities moving forward if only in particles.

One Monday morning I decided to count how many times I was interrupted during the day. I got to forty before I lost track. Interruptions, if thought of as interruptions, can disrupt and fragment life. There have been days when my only goal was to do one job, such as iron five shirts or clean one bathroom or write one letter, and that one job never got done. Children and the telephone cause me the most interruptions.

Knowing about the Law of Particles can help a mother keep sight of her goals if she can find particles of time to do particles of work in many areas of her life. Think of all the things that can be done in particles. I can practice the piano in particles, perhaps by leaving my music open on the piano. I can do a little reading in particles, perhaps by having a magazine or book in the bathroom. I can get my mending done if I leave it ready with needle threaded in the TV room and do it in particles. On the days I feel ambitious or am pushed by deadlines, I use my telephone conversation time to clean out the silverware drawer or unload the dishwasher or wipe up the floor.

Changing a diaper is not an interruption when viewed this way, because one of the most important aspects in a mother's life is to see that her children are well-cared for. A longer than usual phone conversation isn't seen as an interruption; it is a particle of time for a friend who needs to talk.

Knowing and practicing the Law of Particles can give us an element of sanity if we realize that progress is being made on many fronts at least in particles. I am grateful to Joseph Smith for this idea.

Karen: The Law of Substitution

Karen taught me a way of bringing peace to my hectic world. She calls it the Law of Substitution. The basic premise is that the mind can think only one thought at a time, and that good thoughts can supplant bad thoughts. On days when she feels that a large dark cloud is hanging over her and following her around, she disciplines her thought and instead of dwelling on it and magnifying her worries, she consciously substitutes a thought filled with faith or optimism.

One evening not long ago, two of our younger children vomited within five minutes of each other. After I had cleaned them, their clothing, and the furniture, I realized another child was over an hour late coming home from a friend's house. Another child came home and complained because I gave him the wrong kind of sandwich in his lunch sack, and because I hadn't saved dinner for him. Another needed me desperately, instantly, to help hunt for a lost homework assignment, and two others were arguing over who got the piano first. The other one, the only bright light at the moment, was at the bishop's house being interviewed for a patriarchal blessing. But I was even a little worried about him because he'd been there for over an hour. When he came home I knew he had passed the interview because he had the patriarchal blessing form in his hand.

I said, "How was it?"

"Just fine, the bishop is great," he replied.

"What did you talk about all that time?"

"Oh, he just counseled me on school and asked if I were planning a mission and how I was getting along at home. Stuff like that."

"How are you getting along at home?" I asked, needing a little compliment.

"Well . . . well, I told him that right now I was getting along better with my dad than my mom."

He got that reversed, I thought. No mother and son could have a better relationship than we did.

"Don't feel bad, Mom. It's just that right now in my life it's Dad who . . . "

At moments like this, when problems seem to accumulate, causing me to feel inadequate or overwhelmed, I try Karen's trick of substitution. At the moment I feel myself slipping into self-pity or depression, I try substituting in my mind a good memory, thought, or idea to chase the negative feelings away.

One home-economics teacher told me that when bad things begin multiplying in her life, she takes a mental time-out to create something. She said her favorite substitution is to take an old unfurnished apartment and redecorate it in her mind. She carpets the floors, and wallpapers, paints, refinishes wood, chooses furniture and drapes, and hangs original paintings on the walls. This usually helps her unwind sufficiently. Other times she opens a refrigerator in her mind to see what she can fix for dinner.

When I'm feeling steamrollered, I try remembering a special time in my life. For example, when my son told me he had told the bishop that he was not getting along too well with me, I'd practiced enough that I could let the surprising news pass right over me. In this case I quickly substituted a memory of a few nights before when this same son had called me in an urgent voice and asked me to come to his room "to hear some great Baroque music."

Sometimes when a child is misbehaving, I pull the tape of his birth out of my mind and replay the first moments I saw that child. Or I choose any one of the hundreds of happy tapes I have stored in my mind: his first steps, her precious pink-ruffled Easter dress when she was four, the time I was sick on my birthday and she wrapped up every wash cloth in the house and gave them to me for my presents, the time he asked me "What do you think it means to hunger and thirst after righteousness?" These special memories get me through hard moments. I am always ready to click mental photos and put my inner tape recorder on play when special things happen so that I have them stored for future use. These are reruns I love to see.

Margaret: Ensuring a Happy Old Age

When I was a young mother with three little ones, we lived in a large apartment complex in California. All the apartments opened into a courtyard where the swimming pool, walks, flowers, trees, tables, and chairs provided a parklike atmosphere. The children and I spent many happy hours in the courtyard.

One day an elderly woman, whom I knew only as Margaret, came up to me while I was out playing with the children and said, "I watch you and your children from my window, and I know that when you are old, like me, you will still be happy."

"How do you know that?" I asked.

"Because," she said, "you are busy making happy memories for the future. And when you get to be my age, memories are all you've got."

Since then I have tried to build a reservoir of happy memories to help me not only in my old age but every day if necessary. I appreciate this woman who took her time to give me some unsolicited, valuable advice.

Laura: Enduring to the End

Laura told me that about six months after her husband walked out on her she had no desire to get out of bed. She would force herself to get the older children off to school. Then she would let the two preschool children play and she would get back in bed and stay there until forced to get up to take one of the children to the bathroom, to change a diaper, or to fix a sandwich. Finally a moment of reckoning came to her and she thought, "I am going crazy." At that moment she seemed to hear a voice saying, "You have your choice. You can give up and let others take care of you the rest of your life, or you can keep trying and take care of those who are depending on you for support." She was at a crossroads. She realized that giving up was not an option.

She said, "Finding peace in life takes effort. Sometimes in a hectic situation I say to myself, 'Be calm in the midst of this storm,' or 'No matter how unpleasant this moment is, it won't last forever,' or 'The race is not to the swift but to she who endures to the end,' or 'Life was never meant to be easy,' or simply 'Hang in there.'"

She continued, "There is opposition in all things, and free agency, although a divine principle, sometimes causes innocent people to suffer. Events and people are going to turn against us because life was intended to be challenging. Too often we are willing to give up when if we could only see a bit farther down the road, we would be thrilled at what was waiting for us. We should struggle and suffer patiently through the mist and depression of the present to meet the opportunity of the future. If I had given up at this low point in my life, I would never have known the joy of a righteous husband and four more precious, talented, beautiful children."

I wonder how many thousands would rush to apply if advertisements like these were placed in the newspaper: "Wanted: a woman with patience to be the mother of a prophet." "Wanted: a woman to be a mother and a United States senator." "Wanted: a woman to have nine children who will become world-famous entertainers." The truth is, we all answered an ad. We just don't always realize which one. Our advertisement could have read something like these: "Wanted: a woman of endurance who will have two blind children." "Wanted: a woman to raise seven sons alone because her husband will die while still a young man." "Wanted: a mother who is willing to pass through hardship, but her children will all be faithful Latter-day Saints."

I have a neighbor who went to the genealogical library ten years ago to begin the search of her family. To date she has submitted eight thousand names for temple work. How many of us would have answered this ad: "Wanted:

a woman who would like to be a savior on Mount Zion to eight thousand of her kindred dead." We would all have rushed to sign up.

But life is not that way. We have to walk through the tunnel of life to the far edge of the light. Then Heavenly Father moves the light a little farther along. We have to travel the road one step at a time, precept on precept, some days two steps forward, the next day one step back. Hardships, unpleasant situations, difficult choices, illnesses, and accidents are all part of living.

Go forward. Keep hoping. Answer those ads. Don't give up. Believe there are yet good things awaiting you just down the road a few yards or maybe several miles. A loving Father has planned good things for each of his children who endure to the end.

Mother: Music for All Occasions

My mother taught me to use music to create a mood. She always said that if music could soothe the savage beast, it could calm her children as well.

If I feel oppressed and depressed, elated and buoyant, or quiet and pensive, I go to the radio or stereo to find just the right music. I may choose mood music, or classical, or something with a more modern beat. There are even days when I have a craving to hear opera. There are times when I want to make my own music and I will go to the piano to pound out my frustrations by playing loud exercises in twelve keys, or I'll go to the piano to pour out my thanks to God by singing and playing favorite hymns.

There are times I feel like working hard and tunes with a good beat seem to keep me going faster and longer. There are also times when I feel reflective and the radio stations that play old favorites add background to my memories.

Janice: Loving Home

Janice has taught me that home is the most special

place on earth—"second only to the temple," she quali-
fies. Janice is totally happy at home. She makes others
happy when they are in her home. Everyone who visits is
a special guest who is asked to sign a guest register when
leaving. Janice's children and husband have caught her
contagious spirit. They work together to keep the home
continually in readiness for surprise visitors.

After I signed her guest register, I asked her about
her feelings for home. "Well," she philosophically said,
"if you can't be the most happy where you spend the
most time, where are you going to be happy?"

She then took me around her home and showed me
favorite sayings that were strategically placed around the
house. They were all embroidered or written on wooden
plaques in her own calligraphy. I commented on how
beautiful they all were. She said, "I used to do them all
with marker and typepaper. It doesn't matter so much
how they look; it's the message that counts. My walls
talk." That's one reason I enjoy being in her home.

Here are some of her sayings and quotes: "A mother
cannot lead her children closer to God than she is herself." "If you feel dog tired at night, it may be because
you growled all day." "Choices not wishes determine
your fate." "Happiness is an inside job." "Living a good
life is like shaving—no matter how well you do it today,
you still have to do it again tomorrow."

Daniel Webster said, "If we work upon marble it will
perish: if we work on brass, time will efface it: if we rear
temples, they crumble into dust; but if we work upon
immortal minds and instill in them just principles, we are
then engraving that upon tablets which no time will efface,
but will brighten and brighten to all eternity."

And Abraham Lincoln said, "Most folks are as happy
as they make up their minds to be."

Recipe for Preserving Children

1 large grassy field	Flowers
6 small children	Deep blue sky
1 small dog	Narrow strip of brook
Hot sun	with pebbles

"Mix the children with the dog and empty into the field, stirring constantly. Sprinkle the field with flowers, pour the brook over the pebbles. Cover all with a deep blue sky and bake in hot sun. When children are well-browned, they may be removed. Will be just right for setting away to cool in bathtub."

Jackie: Laughing at Yourself

Jackie had a five-day-old baby, a husband who was out of town, and four other children to care for. On this particular evening, she was so exhausted after she had all five children in bed that she hurriedly slipped off her sweater and her slacks and pantyhose together and lay them at the foot of her bed.

The next morning after being up several times during the night, she realized that she had not refilled a prescription that she needed. She got up and put on the sweater and pants that were there on the bed from the night before, stuffed her hair up under a cap, and asked her eleven-year-old child to watch the younger children for a few minutes while she went to the drugstore.

As she walked into the drugstore, the inevitable happened. "Jackie!" a male voice called. There, standing as handsome as ever, was her former high-school boyfriend. She had not seen him in years.

Knowing there was no escape, she thought, "Well, I might not look like my old self, but I still have personality." Jackie put on all her charm and soon was laughing and recalling the fun days of high school. She did notice that several times he looked down at her feet, with a strange look on his face.

Finally he said good-bye, and she turned to go to the back of the store where the pharmacy was located. Suddenly she felt something tugging behind her as she walked. She looked behind her, and to her absolute horror, she saw her pantyhose trailing along behind her. She had forgotten they were inside her slacks from the night before.

She backed up, hoping the pantyhose would somehow magically slide into her pants, but of course, no such luck. She then tried to tuck them up into her pants but to no avail. In desperation she went down an aisle where there were no people, found a ledge to sit on, and pulled and pulled on one leg of the pantyhose until they finally came out.

As Jackie tells the story, tears run continuously down her face—some are from embarrassment, but most are from the hysterical humor of the situation. Obviously, Jackie has a healthy self-esteem that gives her the ability to laugh at herself.

Julie: Leaving Footprints in the Sand

Julie is a saver of things like old report cards, birthday cards, piano recital programs, and so forth. She also likes to write. This combination has created a woman who has taken the challenge to keep histories and journals seriously. Not only does she have her personal history written, not only does she write in her journal weekly, but she also has a complete history written for each of her six children. These histories include memorabilia: hair from the first haircut, samples of the child's handwriting every year, poetry she has written about each child for each birthday.

Julie recently gave a demonstration in Relief Society on how she manages to keep all these histories up to date. She began by quoting a saying that is posted in the genealogical library in Salt Lake City: "A birth certificate proves you were born. A death certificate proves you died. A personal history proves you lived." Then she told us that it has been the writers throughout history who have changed the course of human destiny. To name a few, she mentioned Marx, Darwin, Plato, Nephi, Moses, and Joseph Smith. She then explained her system that allows her, a busy working mother, to keep all these histories up to date.

First, she writes in her own journal at least weekly. In

her journal, she keeps details about her children that she will later want to include in their histories. Second, she keeps a cardboard box in her closet. In the box, she has a file folder for each child, herself, and her husband. Whenever an important school paper, letter, certificate, or newspaper clipping comes along pertaining to a family member, she just drops the item in the appropriate file.

At the end of each year, she extracts all the information on each child from her journal and combines that with the file on each child. She then sits at her typewriter for several hours and writes a synopsis of each child's year, selects the best photos and memorabilia, and puts all this in the child's history. She uses book-of-remembrance binders.

She then displayed her histories. When the oohing and aahing quieted, she said, "Don't be overwhelmed. Keeping these histories is a top priority to me. I am not here to suggest that all of you keep histories just as I do, but I am here to show that it can be done, and that you will gain great satisfaction from doing it."

She told of one evening when things that day had not gone well. She went in her bedroom, got her own history off the shelf and lay down on the bed to reminisce. Before she knew it, it was near midnight. She came back to reality to feel a pillow wet with tears beneath her head. The beauty and pain of her life read as a novel. Peace had replaced the frustration of a few hours before. "Not only was writing these things good therapy for me when I wrote them originally," she said, "but rereading (and reliving) them was just as therapeutic that evening on the bed."

Diane: Taking Control of Whatever You Can

Diane's a woman to envy. She gets up and exercises each morning. She plans her meals a week in advance. She hates to waste time. But whenever anyone comments on what a super-organized mother she is, she says, "Well,

I wasn't always like this. I had to learn from being pushed around by everyone else's demands. One day I realized that if I didn't set up some kind of personal plan to be organized myself, I wouldn't get anything much out of life except more birthdays."

She has learned to set priorities and make lists. She gave me a sample of her version of a things-to-do-today list. It is entitled "Goals + Action = Success." The list is divided into three sections: "Things I Must Do," "Things I Should Do," and "Things I Would Like To Do." She insists that as she does as least a couple of things from the list of things she would like to do, she feels more motivated to get the other things done. She also says that the more she accomplishes, the more she feels she can accomplish. Her view of life is that life is either a vicious cycle or a success cycle.

The vicious cycle could go something like this: Mother is grouchy because she is behind in her work. She angrily asks the children to help her. The children catch the grouchy spirit and are unwilling to help. Mother feels unappreciated and justified in her negative feelings. Mother's attitude becomes more negative. The children become more negative. Mother's self-esteem goes down, on and on in a downward spiral.

On the other hand, if mother can feel success because she made a list of things to do, she may actually accomplish some of the items on the list. If she accomplishes some things, she feels more in control of her life. If she feels more in control, her self-esteem goes up. If her self-esteem improves, her children catch the spirit of doing and accomplishing and their self-esteem increases. Mother is thereby encouraged and makes more lists. She is going onward and upward because success yields success.

Elizabeth: Growing Intellectually

"I am not a very smart person," Elizabeth always says.

"I am just a high-school graduate." But don't let her modest words fool you. She tells that soon after high school, she found herself married with three children. Watching soaps and game shows was her continuing education. "One day," she says, "I was watching a game show. I never before had been concerned that I didn't know any of the answers. But on this day a young mother of three was the contestant. She won for several days. I was so amazed. The master of ceremonies asked her where she got all her knowledge. She answered that she read a lot. 'Hey,' I said to myself, 'I can do that.' Ever since that day, if one of my children asks me a question I don't know the answer to, I say, 'I don't know, but I will find out.' And I do."

Elizabeth takes classes whenever she can. She reads. She goes to concerts and museums. She wants to grow intellectually. If the glory of God is intelligence, she is accumulating gallons of glory.

Sandra: Being the Answer to Others' Prayers

Sandra is one of my all-time favorite people. I admire the fun, creative way she uses her spare time. With any extra time, she tries to be the answer to someone else's prayer.

These are some of the things she does. In the morning, as she takes her daughter to school, she looks for neighbor children who might have missed their bus so that she can give them a ride. She tries to remember the birthdays of everyone in the neighborhood. She is the kind who gives money to the person in front of her in the grocery store line if that person doesn't have quite enough to pay their bill. She prays she will be in the right place at the right time to help her family, friends, ward members, and neighbors when they need her. She does not let others know of her charity; her alms are in secret. We have been friends for so long that I discovered her secret by observation. Then I asked her about what I had observed, and she answered, "I just try to be a tool for my Heavenly Father."

Carol: Leave Your Cape in the Closet

Carol is your average tell-it-like-it-is mother. She does not go all-out for anything, but neither does she miss much of anything. She is truly the salt of the earth.

No one would ever accuse her of having the mother-in-Zion syndrome. You've read about the mother in Zion. Supposedly such a mother never tires, never yells, never feels impatient, depressed, angry, or antagonistic. She is never overwhelmed. She bakes bread and cookies once a day and shares half with her neighbors. She keeps a perfectly organized home. (You know, a place for everything and everything in its place.) She greets her husband each evening at the door with regal charm. The air in her home smells slightly of disinfectants, but mostly of nutritious goodies in the oven. Her children, who are numerous, sit with scriptures open, attentively looking at the speaker every moment of every sacrament meeting. They are well-groomed and proudly wear evidences of mother's ability at the sewing machine. They are honor students and all play musical instruments. (None of them ever has to be reminded to practice.) She never overdraws her bank account and is not an ounce overweight. She can manage any number of Church callings plus hours of weekly volunteer service. She reads the scriptures daily, *U.S. News and World Report* weekly, the *Ensign* and *Smithsonian* monthly, and has a yearly reading list of classics in Church history and doctrine. She not only greets each day with a song but also with vigor.

Carol says that if there are such super moms, she is not even going to try to be one. She refuses to be pressured into competing with her friends in the neighborhood and ward. "What you see is what you get with me," she explains.

For example, last St. Patrick's Day, Carol's three

daughters went to school with a little piece of green construction paper safety-pinned to their socks. Carol was proud of herself for remembering St. Patrick's Day. When the girls got home from school, they told stories of their friends' green. Some had fancy green ribbons in their hair, others had new green barrettes, some had new green undies, one even had fluorescent-green shoelaces. When she told me the story she ended by saying, "Isn't that silly."

Carol is simply not intimidated by others. Isn't that what healthy self-esteem is about? She likes herself just the way she is. When something like St. Patrick's Day happens, her favorite saying is: "Well, I just left my cape in the closet this morning. I didn't want to leap any buildings at a single bound or try to be more powerful than a locomotive."

Carol knows she can't be everything to everyone and rebels at trying. She is the tortoise in the race with the hare. She wins. She is a super mom and person, even without her cape.

I have attempted in this chapter on lessons from my friends to give examples of mothers with specialties. As a people-watcher, I have observed many qualities that I would like to include in my personality and life. Some fit me; some may fit you; and some won't fit at all. But I believe we can learn many things from each other.

TEN

Mothers Who Are
Widowed or Divorced

To prepare materials for this chapter, I interviewed and listened to as many mothers who were single parents as I could. I quickly found that although these mothers are often lumped into one category, to do justice to this important subject, I had to divide the chapter into two sections: mothers who are divorced and mothers who are widowed. Although they have many similar needs, there is one key difference. The divorcée is usually left to fend for herself, whereas the widow usually receives comfort and support from many sources.

Mothers Who Are Divorced

Think of the hub of a spoked wheel. The hub is the woman who is parenting alone. If the woman became single because of the death of her spouse, think of the spokes supporting her from all directions: his immediate and extended family, her immediate and extended family, friends, coworkers, ward members, neighbors, Bible teachings ("Visit the fatherless and the widow in their affliction"), the law (the widow usually receives all that she and her husband had, but the divorcée gets, at best, half), the insurance company, the mortuary staff, the greeting-card companies who make thousands of cards for the widow—but what would a card say to the divorcée?

Now think of the hub as a divorcée. She is often left in an unrealistic suspension without the spokes of a support system. She may be a victim of unsympathetic or gossiping neighbors, who suddenly begin to criticize her if she leaves garbage cans out, if her lawn isn't groomed, or if her children spend time alone in the house. Other spokes that detach themselves include financial security, an intimate other to touch and talk to, and a labor market that views a divorced woman as being temporary or in transition so that promotions and raises go to others.

One of the spokes that no longer supports her is usually her in-laws. This is especially unfortunate when the in-laws have been an integral part of the family's life before the divorce. When their support, love, and attention are gone, the woman feels not only divorced from her husband but also from his family, who also had been her family.

Even well-meaning friends, neighbors, and ward members separate themselves from the divorcée. "Some of the ward members suddenly became distant," was a frequent phrase I heard. "I felt they wanted to be helpful, but they didn't know how. So instead of trying, they avoided me. It was an awkward situation."

Another divorcée said it this way: "Sometime during the first few months after my divorce, I remember someone saying to me that it was not going to be easy to be a divorced woman. They said that single women would not be comfortable around me because I had been married, and married women would not be comfortable around me because I wasn't married. Although this was not always the case, it did not take long to discover that I did not fit into most groups. Even within the Church it became very apparent that most people could not relate to someone who is divorced. No one seemed to be sure how to treat me."

One of the spokes is the children. A divorced mother has to endure increased mother abuse. This makes her a victim in her own home. Children have various ways of

showing their frustration about the divorce, and usually
mother is the one who takes the brunt of it. Instead of
rallying around her and helping her in her time of need,
they often have such insecurities and fears of their own
that they make her life more difficult.

On top of all this separation is the physical burden
of doubled responsibility, doubled workload, and quad-
rupled stress. The divorcée suddenly has to care totally
for the home, the car, the paperwork (like taxes, time
payments, and insurance), the finances, the children,
what to do on holidays, what traditions to keep, the
spirituality in the home, and so forth.

A divorced woman may also victimize herself with
self-defeating behaviors. She may feel burdened with
guilt even when the divorce was not her fault or idea.
She may feel alone and lonely and yet not be willing
to do anything about it. She may spend hours, even
years, in "if only" and "what if" thoughts. She may feel
that she has failed and that there is no hope. Her dreams
are gone. She feels fear, hate, remorse, and especially
rejection. She may wallow in self-pity or have moments
when she is relieved it is all over, vacillating between
highs and lows, peaks and valleys. But the mood is usually deep down in the valley of depression and negative
thoughts. It is no wonder with all this mental, emotional,
physical and psychological turmoil that the divorcée's
self-esteem is low. One divorcée said, "My self-esteem
didn't exist."

Another said, "In the early years after my divorce,
I was not in control of my self-esteem or my emotions.
I was at the mercy of the whims of other people and
situations. My self-esteem depended on whether I had
a good or bad day. If my daughter had a day of misbehaving, or the money wasn't able to stretch as far as
it needed to, my self-esteem dropped. I became a failure
at everything."

And still another said, "At first my bad days out-
numbered the good days, and the good days were just

not enough to build my self-esteem. I could not weather the bad days. I was aware of this at the time but just did not seem to have the control that I needed to turn this around."

The divorcée does not have a flood of visitors expressing sympathy, or cards and letters stating love, or flowers as tangible symbols of concern. Instead, she faces awkward silence and shifted eyes to avoid eye-to-eye contact. She is divorced from most of those support systems she has been accustomed to. She is a victim of an unsuccessful marriage, and everyone and everything seems to pile on top of her while she is down.

After the initial shock wears off, there are stages of adjustment that each divorcée moves through. Sometimes the progress is negligible. There are days, months, or maybe even years when no real progress is felt. During that time, the divorcée must first have hope that there is something to live for and then keep plowing on.

All the above may sound hopeless. But, *if divorce is an end, it is also a beginning.* At a certain point, she will say to herself, "I think I'm going to make it. I think I can cope. I think I am in control once more." When the control comes back, the divorcée is no longer a victim. When she starts to act upon her situation, when the positive begins to overtake the negative, when instead of feeling rejected, she "leans on His ample arm," and when she begins to think outward to help a new divorcée, at that point the divorce becomes an opportunity.

I asked each of the women I interviewed what advice they would give to newly divorced women. Here are their responses:

1. Don't let friendships or opportunities pass you by even if you feel out of place. All people feel awkward at different times. It's how they deal with awkwardness that separates those with low self-esteem and those with high self-esteem. By becoming a part of friendships or organizations, the feelings of being different will soon fade.

2. Don't allow outside forces to control your emotions. Realize that there are going to be days when everything goes wrong and you feel like a failure. But don't give in to these days or these feelings. Have a bad day and enjoy it. At least you are living and experiencing something.

3. Find something that you can succeed at. It doesn't have to be something big. In fact, at first it should be something so small that it is sure to be a success. If you have a desire to start back to school, but it has been ten years and two children since you even read a book, start with one class. After you have had several small successes you can work up to bigger things.

4. As in every period of crisis in life, all of your emotional needs are intensified. Seek supportive friends, especially those who have been there and survived with their self-esteem and their testimony intact.

5. Find service opportunities. I spent one hour each week at a local hospital and my problems seemed to shrink with each visit. I read to patients and wrote letters for them. The loving looks in their eyes rewarded me.

6. In the chaos surrounding divorce, sometimes we neglect those closest to us—our children. Make sure that every day each child has your undivided attention for at least some time. Plan activities with them. Choose a *big* project to accomplish together. Remember, they are having an extremely hard time too.

7. Keep your Church job no matter how busy you think you are. Make it an important experience. Stay close to the Lord.

8. Many turn their attention immediately to getting married again to boost their own self-esteem and show the one who has hurt them that they are attractive to someone else. Usually these relationships only salve wounds and do not heal them. More often than not, the consequences of a hurried decision further compound every existing problem. Take your time getting into a new relationship.

9. Get your mind on other things and give yourself a chance to heal.

10. Find an activity that demands mental alertness.

11. Use this time to find yourself. You will learn who you are. You will grow. I finally got to the level that I knew that if I stayed single forever, it was OK. I had made it!

A woman who is divorced has opportunities to forgive. She has opportunities to forget. She has opportunities for Christlike love.

If she conquers fear, hate, and guilt; if she can learn to be independent and self-sustaining; if she can grow emotionally, spiritually, intellectually, and physically; if she can take control of the eight ball that life has placed in her pocket, she has lifted herself far above what others normally achieve.

I understand that when a bone of the body is broken, the point of fracture actually becomes the strongest place in the bone when it is healed. The divorcée can become stronger than the rest of us when she is healed, because of all she has endured and risen above.

One of the women I interviewed wrote a letter to me describing the progression of her feelings. It read as follows:

"One spring day I returned home to find an unexpected letter from my husband of nearly twelve years—a letter of goodbye.

"At first I had a difficult time coping with anything at all. I wanted to curl up and die. I felt as if my muscles wouldn't work. I knew I could not care for myself and certainly not for my children. I could not even get out of bed. (At least, this is what I thought.)

"The days following the letter were so desperate that I cannot look back on them without the same awful pains returning to my chest, making it difficult to breathe. I didn't want to go on. Every time I managed to go to sleep, I would awaken to the nightmare of realizing all over again what had happened.

"Fortunately, though, no one came to my rescue. I was forced to care for myself and the children. They still needed to be fed and have their laundry done. This was a real blessing because I had to make myself go through the motions of normalcy.

"It was an agonizing effort to take care of my children's needs. I was inconsolable. Surely there was something I could do. My mind darted in every direction trying to grab on to something to make sense of my situation— first hating myself, then hating him for the pain he had inflicted.

"I found that routine was not enough to take my mind off myself. I decided to go back to school. There was a need to force myself to think about other things because the more I dwelt on my own problems, then the longer the wounds stayed open with no chance to heal.

"When nothing was any comfort, I turned to prayer. My Heavenly Father was the only one I felt could understand my grief. He sent the Comforter, and over the days and weeks and months as I prayed, gradually there came a peaceful feeling. At first the feeling came and went. It was as if I were being dragged back from the edge of a precipice, into which if I fell, I would be lost forever.

"Finally this peaceful feeling grew until after about a year, I felt an almost constant radiation of warmth inside. I began to feel new hope, which increased until I felt like praising the Lord continually. I couldn't wait to be on my knees. My life became a constant prayer. This, in spite of problems and overwhelming responsibilities with my children, became a joyful time. I knew I could not take care of the children alone, and He became my constant companion."

If you are not divorced, be grateful. Show your gratitude by going the extra mile for every divorcée you meet. "Bear one another's burden." (Mosiah 18:8.) As I have interviewed these divorcées, my heart has filled with compassion for them. In every case, they do not deserve what life has handed them, but they are striving to make the very best of their future. Do not judge them. Extend the hand of friendship. Be a positive influence in their lives. Try to lift at least one of their many burdens.

If you are divorced, hang in there. Fortunately it does not matter what life does to you, but what you do to life. You really only have two choices: you can give up, let life continue to push you around, and let outside forces determine your self-esteem, or you can force yourself to believe in yourself and, therefore, repair and build your self-esteem.

Mothers Who Are Widowed

Widows are different from divorcées. Calling any woman *single* who was once married and currently is not, no matter what caused her single state, is a mistake. A widow suffers grief, extreme feelings of loss, and goes through the trauma of making a new life for herself, but she usually does not suffer the same devastating blow to her self-esteem that the divorced woman does.

I do not know if a larger sampling of young Mormon widows would confirm my theory, but each widow I talked to was much more at peace with the world and had a higher self-esteem than the women who were divorced. At least, the recovery time for divorcées appears to be longer.

The widows who responded to my questionnaire seem to have a special feeling that perhaps God had allowed them to become widowed for a specific purpose. They seem to be anxious to discover what that purpose is and work out their problems to the best of their ability. This is not to say that there aren't periods of self-pity, depression, and overwhelming stress because of the workload and responsibility. That would be an understatement. But they seem to have an undercurrent of ultimate faith to see them through. Here are some responses that illustrate that faith:

Linda: "At first when the realization hit me that I was

alone, the feeling was one of fright and worry and of being incapable of doing everything alone. I have never considered myself single, however. I still feel married and become very resentful when I receive literature from the special interest group. That may seem strange to others, but I am still married. As I have worked hard and as the time since Eric's death has increased, life has progressed and my self-esteem has risen to probably a higher level than before I was widowed. I now see that I can do it. I can manage alone—not that it's pleasant."

Marcie: "After the funeral I was anxious to get back to our home and keep my family unit intact. I didn't want to become an extension of my parents' family. I wanted to be home with my little family. I felt that if there was a place Dave's spirit would come, it would be to our home. I wanted to keep things as much the same for the children as possible. I wanted their routine to be back to normal quickly."

Patti: "My own will to survive and make the best of every situation has been a help to me. I determined to be happy, and that comes from my testimony that there will be a reunion with my family someday. I feel Bob is just away on a trip . . . he seems close. I do not feel terrible anguish and loneliness, but then I have family around and a very full schedule every day. I try to keep busy at night too, but nights are the worst."

I asked these women, "What are the hardest things about being widowed?" They answered as follows:

Tara: "My biggest problem with being a single parent is that I have no one to discuss any problems with. The decisions I make weigh heavily as to whether they are right or wrong. I try to ask myself how Tom would have handled the situation."

Patti: "Sometimes it is hard to look at couples and at my friends who are having babies. I occasionally have to force myself to be happy for them."

Marcie: "The twenty-four-hour-a-day responsibility is sometimes just too much. At first, I didn't even have a way to say, 'Take the children for an hour and let me take a bath.' Little things—even going to the store—seemed like a big deal."

Linda: "It is hard to find other singles my age. There really aren't a lot of young widows. The girls who were divorced or never married—well, we just don't have a lot in common. I am more comfortable with the friends I already had."

Tara: "I don't really have anyone I can talk to who understands. I think that's because I put up a front like everything is fine. I think I have to be a superwoman to everybody. I don't want it to show when I'm depressed because that is like soliciting sympathy. That's not helpful because people give you too much. I just never let my barriers down."

Patti: When you are so used to having a constant companion, it's hard to ask someone to do something with you. Many times I would rather go shopping alone or to a concert alone, for instance, than go to the trouble of asking someone to go with me."

Tara: "It is hard to be in groups when the ladies are talking about what their husbands are doing. I come home burdened by that sometimes. I don't know what my husband is doing, and the ladies would be uncomfortable if I expressed what I think he is doing in the spirit world. But then I say to myself, 'Hey, you can't feel bad about loving someone and missing him.'"

Linda: "I miss the sweet, complimentary things my husband used to say to me. That is gone. It is easy for me to get discouraged because I don't get complimented any more."

Marcie: "When I finally was persuaded that I should date, I set myself up for many discouraging times. Blind

dates are the pits. One guy called and said his family was
making him call me, that he was under a lot of pressure
to take me out. So, he wanted to get it over with as soon
as possible. I did go out with him. I can't believe now that
I patronized him. Another said he wouldn't take me out
until he had seen me. He came over, left his car running,
came to the door, took one look at me, and then walked
out. He never did ask me out. At the time it really hurt.
Now I see how funny it was."

Linda: "Lots of people are inspired as to whom I'm
supposed to marry. It's never that they feel I might have
a fun date or a nice time or friendship. No, it's always
that they have had it revealed to them the man I am supposed to marry. Those kinds of things are shattering. I
wonder why I have to be exposed to all of this. Those
times would shake me up. Then I'd have to stabilize myself again."

I also asked, "What helped you adjust to your situation?"

Marcie: "I needed time to myself. I took time to
grieve. I kept track of my feelings in my journal."

Tara: "At the time of my husband's death, the Spirit
of the Holy Ghost was constantly with me; it carried me
through the funeral. After the funeral, when I didn't
feel the Spirit with me all the time, I'd always compare
myself to those times I felt such peace and joy. Then I'd
feel guilty about being down. I'd think, 'Why can't I sustain that peaceful feeling? I must not be a very good
person if I can't remember all those neat things and
maintain an eternal perspective.' The minute I'd feel depressed, I'd feel guilty and that would just depress me
more. It took me a while to allow myself that down time
and say to myself, 'It's OK.'"

Linda: "I went to some lectures for single mothers
and learned how to manage the stress that comes from
feeling overwhelmingly responsible for everything. I

found that I didn't have to do everything all at once. I was in charge, and I didn't have to feel pressure from others if I didn't want to."

Patti: "Some people were so gushy with sympathy that I couldn't stand it. Others acted like I didn't deserve any sympathy. Like my dad. He would always say things like, 'Who do you think you are, someone special? Get up and get going.' He would let me know I wasn't going to get any sympathy from him. He always pulled me up by my bootstraps. From him I could take it. It really helped."

Marcie: "So often I'd see all the things I didn't have instead of all the things I did. I had to make lists of my blessings. So often I felt overwhelmed with the things I wanted and needed but couldn't change. Making lists of blessings helped me."

Tara: "Writing in my journal when I was feeling really up was a great help. Then I could go back to those places in my journal and see I was way up there once. If I got there once, I could do it again. I know exactly where the ups are written. My journal falls open to them."

Linda: "My greatest source of spiritual strength came from going to the temple. I felt a closeness, a peace, a promise of reunion."

Next, I asked, "What advice would you give to new widows, and what would you do differently if you had it to do over again?"

Marcie: "If I had to do it again I would definitely be more selfish in that I would consider my education and my needs as important as my husband's and children's. I would try to prepare for the possibility that I might be a widow. I think someone called it *widow preparedness.*"

Linda: "The advice I would give to newly widowed women would be to get involved in hobbies, school, helping others—anything to keep too busy to dwell on yourself."

Patti: "Long before a woman becomes widowed, she should prepare herself for the eventuality. Know everything about your husband's business or profession—the financial end of things. Know about your insurance, where his will is, how to run the business of the family before you have to do it by yourself. Learn about money and how to manage it. Your husband might not want you to know about all these things and may say he doesn't want you to worry your pretty little head about it . . . but believe me, it will be more of a worry afterward if you don't know anything about insurance, legalities, and finances."

Tara: "At the funeral the bishop said, 'Trust in the Lord. He is fair. This may not seem fair to you right now, but you will be compensated. The rules of life are fair, but sometimes you have to wait into the eternities to understand the reasons.' Every time I feel down, I try to remember and believe those words."

The last question I asked was: "Are there any compensations right now, in this life, to being a widow?"

Linda: "I think I have been truly blessed with wonderful health and strength to accomplish the almost impossible right now. The insurance money paid the mortgage and gives us enough each month that along with my part-time work, we will be just fine. My job is pleasant. My prayer is that I can carry on long enough to get each of the children safely on their feet. Yes, I feel I am watched over a little bit more than married women, by my Father in Heaven and by my family and by the ward."

Patti: "I feel His grace compensates. I think widows get extra help. I know I'm not different from anyone else except I have greater needs. So I receive more help."

Tara: "I'm afraid I have painted a rosy picture. Well, it is not easy being a widow, not any part of it. But I am not angry anymore. I trust my Heavenly Father. I feel much more dependent on him than I used to. In that way, it has been worth all the grief and pain and trouble. I am in his hands. If we had been separated because of a miserable divorce, that would be a tragedy. But we are just separated for a time. It is not a tragedy, just an awesome inconvenience."

Marcie: "One night I was so desperate. I had never struggled with prayer before. I admitted to Heavenly Father that even though I had so many blessings, I had so many weaknesses and was having such a difficult time adjusting. I was very specific. I had been given so much but I was struggling. That night, on my knees, the Spirit came to me so strong. It was total friendship, total love. I'd never experienced anything like it before—but then I never had had the urgency and need before.

"The things he told me that night were to press forward. Then I was told seven things I was to do, that I should accomplish. I remember mentally writing them down. The prayer was really long. The Spirit was so strong. I didn't want to say amen because I knew the Spirit would leave and it would be reality again.

"I wrote down the seven things the next day. They were the things the prophet has told us over and over. I remember when I received them I thought, 'This is so personal, so significant.' But then I saw they were what I knew all along: saying daily prayer, reading daily scripture, eating right, exercising, having family home evening, getting to Church meetings, and having special activities and vacations with the children. So the gospel applies to everybody. The principles work for everybody no matter what the situation. I am grateful Heavenly Father saw fit to reveal them to me in my time of greatest need."

The eleven points of counsel given by divorcées also apply in large measure to the widow as she builds a new life for herself.

ELEVEN

Mothers Who
Work Outside the Home

I recall the hectic days when I worked. I remember leaving at six-thirty each weekday morning to take our two children to the babysitter and then driving to the junior or senior high school where I taught. I remember the total exhaustion. I remember having morning sickness (actually it was all-day sickness) and trying to teach English to 206 seventh and eighth graders. I remember mustering any reserve energy to have clean shirts for Richard, diapers for the children, and to teach the Young Women in our ward. I remember feeling divided and subdivided and only about fifty percent effective.

What effect does working have on a mother's self-esteem? (The term *working* is used loosely in this chapter to mean employed outside the home. We all know mothers do almost nothing but work, whether employed or not.) To answer this question, I sent out questionnaires and interviewed women who were working outside their homes, working from their homes, and not working. I have come up with a not-too-scientific but very interesting survey. This chapter and the next will have quotations from my interviews with about twenty mothers.

The first question I asked was this: "Do you work outside the home or have a home-based job? If so, please explain why you work. If you do not work, please explain

your reasons for not working." As I analyzed and cate-
gorized the answers, I ranked these working women by
level of job satisfaction and overall self-esteem.

Group One: The most dissatisfied group (a small per-
centage, maybe six percent) were those mothers who are
the only means of support for their families: divorcées,
widows, women who have to suddenly return to work because their husbands have become disabled. The women
in this group have few job skills and spend hours in bor-
ing, low-paying jobs. These women are more inclined to
feel monumental pressure and blame most of their frustrations in life on the fact that they must work to keep
food on the table and clothe their children.

One woman wrote: "My ex pays alimony and child
support only now and then. I have to work. I feel I am
being punished over and over. I would never have chosen
to work. I am the stay-at-home type. I work long hours
for little better than minimum wage. I didn't go to college
or anything."

Although six percent were dissatisfied with their job, I
found several women in this category—sole means of support for their families—who had high self-esteem. The
variable I found between these women and those who
were highly dissatisfied was the amount of education or
training that they had. It appears a higher job level means
greater job satisfaction and more self-esteem.

Group Two: The next most pressured group is the
typical young mother, like the description I gave of myself at the beginning of the chapter. One hassled young
mother said: "I work for survival. My husband is in
school and will be for three more years. My earnings
barely cover tuition and family needs. I hate working, because our two children get left each day at a neighbor's. I
have to work, care for the children, do the housework,
shopping, and everything else myself. My husband tries
to be supportive but really does nothing but study. I love
him and am willing to make this sacrifice, but it is hard."

Group Three: The largest majority of mothers work for financial reasons, as in groups one and two. Group three is no different in that respect; however, these contented working women provide a second income that supplements their husband's earnings. They have found that two incomes are necessary for the basics or to maintain a higher life-style than his alone would allow.

These mothers are mostly thirty to fifty years of age. Many of them were stay-at-home mothers during the early years of raising children. As needs increased and the husband's income did not rise proportionately, mother went to work. The attitude of these women about working is philosophical. They feel that it is the season in life to work and balance home responsibilities. Most said that they enjoy the added challenge. Some of their replies were as follows:

"My husband's job does not provide enough money. I have to work so I have some funds I can control. I would love to stay at home and be the mother my mother was. I see now that her life—being able to stay at home and be a wife and mother—was a luxurious state."

"I work outside of the home and have always worked outside the home for financial reasons. Basically, the profession my husband has is a job of peaks and valleys and does not pay enough money to meet the requirements of a growing family. It has taken two paychecks to furnish us with the basics of life."

"I sat down one day and made a chart of each child and where they would be in a few years and what they would be doing. In looking at the chart, my husband and I realized we would have all these children in high school, on missions, and in college at the same time. We knew we would need additional income to manage. Rather than have my husband work two jobs—as we had done once before—we decided I should go back to work. I had a profession, had graduated from college, and had something to contribute that was needed."

Group Four: The next group (a much smaller group,

maybe fifteen percent) were mothers who could stay at home if they wanted to be very frugal and have life remain static. These mothers expressed themselves in optimistic terms. I noticed that, as with everything else in life, if a person chooses to do something, it always seems to be more pleasant than if he or she is forced. These women have chosen to work. Note the difference in their responses from the mothers in the first two groups:

"I work for several different reasons. As my children began to get older I began to worry about my identity. By working I am something other than someone's mother or someone's wife. Also I feel that I owe something to society. It is very valuable for my self-esteem. I also feel I need something to challenge my intellect and talents."

"I went back to work to gain a sense of competence and of being useful. As the children got older I had a sense of personal urgency to make a decision either to return for my degree or face years ahead of what I perceive to be little personal growth. Another, although less weighty reason for working was to have some funds over which I had control, and as time went on, contribute to our retirement."

"I work because I like the freedom my own money brings and because this is the way we have been able to do home improvements and vacations that we wouldn't have otherwise had."

Group Five: This next group is fascinating. These women stay at home but still produce income. They are mothers who operate home-based businesses. I interviewed a mother who has a full-fledged candy factory in her home, and another mother who runs a billing service for several doctors. One makes $1,200 a month teaching piano lessons. Others have preschools in their homes, teach tole painting and other crafts, tend children, freelance as artists or writers, and even make truant calls for a local high school. This is a very busy, content group.

One woman expressed her feelings this way: "If I worked full-time or even part-time with regular hours, it would interfere with my ability to be the kind of wife, mother, and homemaker I desire to be. My family comes first. I also enjoy being my own employer and controlling my own degree of involvement and what hours I work. I am now producing a product that yields twenty dollars an hour. I find that when I am busy with one of my ventures, I become more organized and get more done in less time than when I am not busy with one of the projects."

Group Six: This final group is nearly on the endangered species list—the traditional stay-at-home mother. These mothers can stay at home for one of two reasons. Either the husband makes ample money, or the husband makes adequate money and, with frugality, an added income is not necessary. Very few of the mothers have consciously chosen to stay at home. Things just worked out that way so they could.

Stay-at-home mothers can add stability to neighborhoods and wards. These are the mothers who can run the PTA. These are the mothers who can bandage skinned knees of the neighborhood children whose mothers are at work. These are the mothers who can keep alive the traditional image of mother.

Now that we've identified the different groups of women, let's look at the answers to the next question I asked: "Does working affect your self-esteem?" The following quotations are a sampling of the answers I received:

"High self-esteem only comes through satisfaction of a job well-done in career or home. I feel I have grown in confidence, realizing I can accomplish most tasks I put my mind to."

"As one meets so many challenges and 'stays on top' it couldn't help but have a positive influence on self-esteem."

"Yes. I feel my job as mother, wife, and homemaker

is most important, but I also feel that by making use of my education and technical experience, I am contributing something to the community where there is a need that just anyone is not trained to fill."

"I am not so sure that it is my career that has given me high self-esteem or if it is obtaining goals that I have laid out for myself."

"Just knowing I could go back to school, get a job, and be successful has raised my feeling of self-worth. I also feel my children are proud of me. Even my name on the monthly check gives me more value in my own eyes."

"To a point it has. It is nice to be able to go out and meet with people other than your children. It is also nice to be able to enjoy the profit of your labor."

"Working is just one more thing I have to cope with. It complicates my life. I never have a moment to myself. I don't think my self-esteem can be healthy with so many draining responsibilities."

About three-fourths of the women I surveyed felt that their self-esteem was healthier because they could manage a job *and* their home responsibilities. The others felt working had little to do with self-esteem or was an added complication.

The next question asked was this: "What effect has your employment had on your children?" About seventy-five percent expressed that working has been more positive than negative for their children. Many mentioned their children were more responsible than children whose mothers stayed at home.

One woman said: "The best thing that ever happened to my children was for me to go to work. I had been an overprotective mother. If one of my children forgot a lunch or an assignment, I would race to the school to get it to him. Now if one of them forgets, there is no one at home to answer the phone. It has been amazing how few things the children have forgotten."

Other working women mentioned their children expressed greater security because they knew mother could earn a living; some felt the conversations at the dinner table were of higher quality because of mother's experiences at work; others felt the children had been more interested in school because they had seen the correlation between school and the amount of money that could be earned.

However even these mothers who felt working was more positive than negative expressed some problem areas:

"When my mother found out I was going back to work, she said, 'Leave the home and your children will end up in Hell.' I hope she is not right, but my being out of the home so much has caused problems. The children are much more on their own and do experiment when left to themselves so much."

"When things go smoothly it is great sailing, but when there are rough seas, watch out. I have missed many of the children's school events, and I've missed the more casual and leisurely conversations we could have had if I weren't always so busy."

"My biggest problem is that by the time I get home from work, I am really tired. When I get home I have to worry about getting dinner ready, keeping the house picked up, and spending the time with my children they want and need."

"A working mother misses out on her children's daytime school activities and luncheons when mothers are invited. All domestic activities suffer: cooking, sewing, crafts, and so forth. Mother is not home when children come home from school. If a child is sick, mother has to make a big choice: she can send the child to school sick, stay home with the child and lose a day's pay, or leave the child home alone. There is more emotional stress because both parents are trying to wear two hats."

One mother said she missed being able to sit with her children at the piano as they practiced. Another said all music lessons stopped because the children would not spend the time without her encouragement. Another said, "One daughter felt less loved because I could no longer make her clothing." She felt she missed some pampering. An older daughter developed a serious TV habit, which her mother blames on the fact that she was not at home after school to supervise activities.

It is easy to blame every little problem in the home on the fact that mother works. I doubt, however, that this is true. There would be problems if she stayed at home. We need to find what problems are related to the fact that mother works; then solutions can be found.

The other evening while I waited for a child in the library, I read through about six magazine articles on the consequences of mothers working. In that hour I read several articles in which experts expressed concern that latch-key kids, those who let themselves into their homes after school because their mothers are at work, have a greater chance of drug abuse, sexual experimentation, interest in pornography, truancy, poor performance in school, obesity, excessive TV watching, and even teenage suicide. Of course, these problems occur even when mother is at home, but the statistical evidence shows that the children who have stay-at-home mothers are not as likely to have these problems.

There can be little argument that stay-at-home mothers have the opportunity to have a more active role in their children's lives. If mother maximizes this time, the children are the benefactors. However, if mother is always at the club, out shopping, or in front of the TV watching the soaps, she is not as beneficial.

Next I asked the working mothers this question: "What are the problems associated with having a job and trying to be a good mother?" They responded with honesty.

"I always feel that I am behind. I never get caught up with the tasks at hand. There is never time enough to do the things I would like to do. I always feel guilty because I do not visit enough with parents, friends, and other family members."

"Working takes a lot of energy, so I do have to delegate chores. At times I have to close my eyes on work done by the children, because I know that I would have done better. Another problem is that if I were home, many things would be done that I just don't find time for. Sometimes I have a guilt hand-up over things left undone."

"Trying to keep up with all of the housework and washing and clothing needs, when I work fifty hours a week and have only Saturday to handle the home chores, is nearly impossible. Meeting the needs of family, church, community, and home when there are so many demands on my time causes me to resent everything. Keeping the balance and priorities straight is difficult. The children don't feel the need to get things done like I do. I get little time for reading, study, attending a play, or anything else—except work and housework. My extra time goes to the Church and kids."

"Fatigue is the biggest problem. I am too tired for a lot of things. I really am exhausted most of the time. Events and things have to be pretty high on my list of priorities to get done. My house isn't as clean and laundry stacks up. I don't read as much. I don't pursue hobbies as I once did. I don't know where my children are every minute like I did before I went back to work."

"Time and emotional energy are all used up in the eight hours at work. There is little left at the end of the day for husband and children."

After reading the responses of these women, it seems that the working mother probably has more stress, more fatigue, and more mother abuse than her nonworking counterparts. What consequences lie in the future for the children of working mothers? How can the working mother keep her self-esteem healthy? Are there solutions? For answers to these and other pertinent questions, stay tuned and read chapter 12.

TWELVE

Solutions to
Working Mothers' Problems

The final question I asked in the interviews was: "Do you foresee any problems in the future because mothers work?" I have organized the responses into five sections to highlight the problems. Possible solutions follow each problem.

Problem: Future Crisis

"I loved staying home with my children when they were small. I'm not so sure my daughters will have that luxury. One problem I foresee is how we can get our young women to prepare for an occupation. There are many of them, at the ripe old age of eighteen or nineteen, who think it is time to settle down and have a family. They only think of marriage and motherhood. I firmly believe we must do more to prepare our young ladies to take care of themselves by learning skills that they can utilize should the need present itself, which all of us know happens frequently.

"For my daughters I would hope that they are well prepared in a profession before they have children, not because I don't want them to be first and foremost wives and mothers, but rather because I see that more and more mothers work. That doesn't mean it is right. I just think there is a future crisis lurking if our young women don't understand that the chances are about fifty-fifty that they will have to work."

94

Solution: Prevent Crisis

As I look to the future, I, too, worry about our daughters really more than about us. If the trend continues, and there is every reason to believe it will, more and more of our daughters will be working mothers. I see this as a critical issue of our time and a potential problem that can be avoided for many of our young women.

I think we, mothers, need to teach our daughters to prepare for careers. They must prepare with whatever training or education it takes after high school so they will have specific marketable skills. The time may come when they will need a job to meet financial needs, and they will want it to bring as much personal satisfaction as possible. Each young woman needs to know that "happily ever after" may include the death of her husband, divorce, financial reverses, or maybe no husband at all.

These facts may be helpful in getting their attention:

1. Ten percent of LDS women who are between the ages of eighteen and thirty will be widowed before age sixty.
2. Thirty-five percent will be divorced before age sixty.
3. Three percent will never marry.
4. Forty-five percent will be the primary breadwinner in their homes before age sixty-five. (See *Church News,* 6 November 1983, p. 4.)

Another survey released in 1980 "showed that thirty-four percent of LDS women work outside the home, and that fifty-seven percent did so to meet basic living expenses. Another thirty-five percent were working because they were widowed or divorced; seventeen percent said they needed involvement and self-expression outside the home; and eight percent said they were career women." (*Deseret News,* 13 February 1983.)

Other statistics indicate nine out of ten women in the United States will work outside their homes at some point in their lives. (L. C. Chenowith and E. Maret, "The

Career Patterns of Mature American Women," *Sociology of Work and Occupations,* 1980, pp. 222-51.) Another study showed that an average twenty-four-year-old woman would spend forty-five percent of her life in the labor market. ("Women at Work," U.S. Bureau of Labor Statistics, Bulletin 2168, April 1983, p. 12.)

I think the message is clear. We need to help our young women prepare for the future. If they don't prepare, and if circumstances force them into the labor market, they will likely be employed in low paying, dead-end jobs that women traditionally occupy. About eighty percent of women in today's work force are employed in jobs that pay low wages.

I call the years between twelve years of age and the day a young woman marries, her "years of preparation." We need to help each young woman prepare for her highest career level. Our aim in doing so is not to detract from her important calling as wife and mother, but to enhance it and to help her meet the future successfully if she needs to support herself and her family.

We must help our high-school girls see that social experiences are not more important than scholastic achievement or career preparation. The choices a girl makes during the critical and crucial preparation years will determine her quality of life for the rest of her life. The more productive her years of preparation are, the more able and happy she will become.

Too many young women think they are waiting, biding time until Prince Charming comes along. Young women might be better prepared for marriage, motherhood, and a possible career if they would realize how high the chances are that they will work. Then they would plan and equip themselves for a career according to their interests, talents, and abilities. They would learn self-sufficiency and independence. Then when ninety-seven percent of them do marry, they will be ready for any eventuality. Each young woman must know that if she does marry and never works a day in her life, career

preparation will still be one of the most valuable invest-
ments she could have made. She will have extra skills
with which to bless her family. As a consequence, her
self-esteem will be healthy, and she will feel secure knowing the insurance policy she took out on herself during
her years of preparation is there for her just in case she
needs it.

Problem: Unprepared Mothers

"So often I see mothers who seem surprised to find
themselves needing a job. They haven't given any
thought or preparation to where they will work or who
will care for their children. I think women need to think
ahead to the needs of the future whenever possible."

Possible Solution: Plan Ahead

In the first problem, the need for young women to
prepare to avert a personal crisis in the future was discussed. Many of the women I interviewed expressed concern about today's mothers. The same principles are true
whatever the age of the woman. If you are not currently
working, you may want to prepare for the day when you
might need to. If you already have a marketable skill, it
would be to your advantage to keep that skill polished
and ready to use. You might also take an occasional class
or read about the latest advances in your field. It is wise
to prepare now, before you need to use your skills in the
marketplace.

If you do not have a marketable skill you would enjoy
using daily, plan to obtain one. Assess your educational
background. List your interests, aptitudes, and talents.
Decide how you can obtain a marketable skill with the
least amount of money, time, and stress. Now is the time
to begin.

Prepare for a variety of possible situations. What
would you do if it becomes necessary to work full-time?
Do you have talents and skills you could use to earn
either a part-time or full-time wage while at home? What

home-based occupations might you consider? What pro-
visions will you make for your children's care? Do you
really need more money or just want more? Would making do and doing without solve the financial problem?

Problem: Trapped by Long Hours and Low Pay

"In my department there are about fifty women who
are first-level secretaries. I know that most of them are
mothers. They spend eight hours a day five days a week
working for just a little better than minimum wage. I
think most of them could do better."

Possible Solution: Improve Job Skills and Consider Alternatives

If you are now in a situation where you must work, do
you find your job financially, intellectually, and spiritually satisfying? Are there good opportunities for advancement? Do you have a career plan? How can you upgrade
your occupational skills? Do you feel that you are making
a difference in the workaday world?

If you have to work, decide what is the most important benefit of that job. Is it most important to work close
to home? Is it important to work only while the children
are in school? Do you need a high-paying job? Do you
need employee benefits (like insurance) more than anything else? Are you looking for a job with excellent opportunities for advancement, or one with little stress, or
one that is superchallenging? Any woman can go out and
find any old job, but it is like buying a dress. If the job fits,
the mother will be much happier. She should consider
training for a job she will like rather than taking the first
job that is available.

Here are some case studies showing alternative ways
to solve similar problems.

When Maurine, a thirty-year-old mother of three, was
divorced, she could have found a clerical or light-industry
job for immediate money. Instead, she returned to the

university to complete her nursing degree. Although it took nearly three years of living solely on alimony and child support, she now is happily employed at a hospital doing what she loves.

Grace, a thirty-seven-year-old mother of six, found the demands of a big family were stretching the family's budget beyond its limits. As bills began to pile up, the stress on the family increased. Wishing to remain at home while contributing to the family income, she obtained a business license and opened a beauty shop in her home.

Yvonne is a sales representative for a product sold at parties. She makes deliveries several times a week, but can handle all her other business transactions by phone. Her family hardly knows she is employed. She has added income to keep her family solvent.

Liz, who taught kindergarten before she was married, missed being a teacher but didn't want to leave her small children. She and her husband bought some used school equipment and set up a preschool in their basement. Seven years later, her preschool has such an excellent reputation that she has a long waiting list.

Laurel was unable to have children for the first five years of her marriage. While she waited and hoped for a family, she finished her undergraduate work and then obtained her master's degree. Twelve years and six children later, Laurel was left alone with those six children. Fortunately, she was able to secure a teaching job at the university. She feels greatly blessed to have been prepared.

Problem: Using Work as an Escape

"I foresee that some mothers will not be very successful in their home life. Their children may not be turning out very well, so instead of staying at home and resolving the problems, they will go to work. This is an escape. The more time they spend away from home, the less they feel responsible for what is going on there. I worry about how their daughters are going to learn to be good mothers if the role model is never home."

Possible Solution: Set Priorities

This solution is for the working mother who is happy in her job and whose future looks secure and bright. The solution is to keep your priorities straight. I know from the writing I do, that it is easy to become so immersed in a project that children, husband, and home slide into the background. I have been guilty—especially when meeting deadlines—of looking at the children when they speak to me, but not hearing a word.

Today, I did just that. I was deep in thought when my five-year-old son came in and told me something. I looked at him, eye to eye, but was thinking, *working mothers . . . self-esteem . . . solutions . . .* "That's nice," I said, giving him a little hug and smile. "Why are you smiling?" he asked in a shocked voice. "I just told you darts and arrows can kill people." I'm sure his five-year-old brain was registering, "My mother is all wrapped up in her writing. She is not listening to me. Her writing is more important than me."

I tell myself to remember that I can be a writer all of my life, but I can be the mother of five-year-old Daniel for only one year. I need to keep my priorities straight.

One of the working mothers I interviewed explained how she keeps priorities in their proper order. She says that she is either so involved in her work that she is anxious to get to work, or the problems at work are so pressing that she can't get them out of her mind. Before she discovered her solution, she was turning into a robot-like mother—there in body but not in mind. Then one night when she was reading the TV log, she noticed that *Dr. Jekyll and Mr. Hyde* was on. Just reading those words reminded her of how she was at home—Dr. Jekyll at home and Mr. Hyde at the office. She vowed that this would stop. Now when she leaves work, she symbolically takes off her work hat and leaves it there. As she drives in the driveway, she puts on her wife-and-mom hat. She says a silent prayer as she turns off the engine and walks to the house: she prays that she can be a wife and mother in body, mind, and spirit.

Problem: Mother's Two Hats Too Heavy

"Fathers need more training to help in housework and with children. The world is changing too much to stick with father being handed the paper and his slippers. If the woman is doing about ninety percent of the work with the house and children plus holding down a job, she will feel resentment. A family needs a happy mother."

Possible Solution: Training Father

Traditional homes where father brings home the bacon and mother stays at home can play a mean trick on mother when she becomes employed outside the home. Usually father continues to work at his job and helps out at home like nothing has changed. The working mother must work at her job plus do all she was doing before. That adds up to about two forty-hour jobs a week. Add to that the fact that mother's work is never done and that she is on call twenty-four hours every day, including holidays and Sundays, and her stress and fatigue level may bubble over the top.

Several solutions may be tried. Even though I have not been technically employed for many years, I still spend many hours each week writing. I have needed help to maintain the home. I soon discovered that it is not in most husband's job description to analyze what they can do each day to help with the housework and children. So, I finally just told Richard that I needed his help. He said that he would do whatever I needed if I would just make him a list. It has worked well. True, sometimes I make a long list and it doesn't all get done. I still know that I am receiving help, and the most urgent things do get done. This week I needed a leaky tap repaired and help balancing the bank statement. He also will help with dishes, homework, transportation to and from lessons, and nighttime preparations like tooth-brushing, stories, and prayers.

Husbands should not be expected to be mind readers when it comes to knowing exactly what jobs need doing. If a wife waits for her husband to sense her needs, she may wait indefinitely. I recommend that you simply ask for the help you need.

I also suggest that you share with your husband any information that you learn about being an effective parent. Although there are no Father Education classes during priesthood meetings, you can teach your husband many things that you have learned during the Mother Education lessons in Relief Society. For years after every Mother Education class, I have gone home and given the lesson to Richard!

Last Thoughts on the Subject

When I think of today's mothers—working, mothering, struggling, trying—I think, "Well, we will make it. We women are great. We are creative. We can manage so much. Most of us rise to whatever challenges we meet."

I like to read about the first working mother described in the Bible. I am referring to the passage in Proverbs about the virtuous woman. She not only cooks and sews for her family but also runs businesses: real estate and making girdles. She dresses like royalty. She gets up before dawn. She takes care of the poor. She opens her mouth and wisdom floats out; she is never idle; she is always kind; and she fears the Lord. (See Proverbs 31.)

I don't think working is necessarily the ideal or that any mother should seek employment, but if a woman has to work, I believe she will make it work. I have confidence in women.

Secondly, as I read history from the earliest of times, through the pilgrims and past the pioneers, I see that women have sacrificed all through the history of the world. Women have worked hard in every century. Maybe having to work in the twentieth century means being employed or running a business from your home as well as being a homemaker. Perhaps this is our current type of sacrifice. We have many modern conveniences that make life easier than ever before in the history of the world. Is this our challenge—to use these wonderful conveniences to the fullest so that we have time for work, home, children, husband, church, community, and ourselves?

As I come full circle in defining the role of today's working woman, I see that the working woman has problems to face that are unique to her situation. But she also has opportunities. Working can be a mixed blessing. I feel that the most important factor is the attitude of each individual. It's each mother's self-esteem that determines her ability to cope.

Yesterday I met an eighty-five-year-old woman who was taken out of school when she was eight years old to work as a maid in a hotel. She has been employed nearly every day since. She has outlived two husbands, has raised seven children, and is an absolute joy to be around. She has a basement full of projects that she is saving for her old age.

Many mothers will have to work most of their lives. Opportunities sometimes literally come in work clothes. Maybe this is our refiner's fire. If we can develop the cheerful outlook and charming personality of this lovely eighty-five-year-old woman I met yesterday, we will have as many rewards as sacrifices.

THIRTEEN

Is Anyone Building
Mother's Self-Esteem?

A few days ago I cleaned out a drawer and found two lists of blessings I wrote years ago. The first list was written at the end of a particularly trying and unproductive day. It read: "There was no earthquake today. The house did not burn down. No one got run-over." I smiled at the memory.

The second list, written at the end of a wonderful, everything-fell-into-place day, included all the blessings you would expect to find on such a list: the gospel, peace in our nation, a living prophet, scriptures, a good marriage, fine children, a strong body, ancestors who accepted the gospel, money to provide for our needs, and on and on.

As I looked at the two lists, I thought how good contrast is. What a marvelous plan Heavenly Father has placed in motion where we can know good from evil, pleasure from pain, and have good days and bad. He knew that without change we would cease to appreciate the good. As bleak as a bad day is, we can endure because we have experienced better days and know brighter times will come. A philosophical friend of mine says, "If you can't be thankful for what you receive, at least be thankful for what you escape."

Recently I listened to the words of a prayer, "We thank thee for all the blessings we endure." I'm sure the word meant was *enjoy*, but endure is often accurate. Children are blessings that we must endure on occasion. Church callings are blessings we may have to endure. Home, garden, kitchen, food, and husband can all be blessings that we endure at times.

Endurance is the ultimate test. The thirteenth Article of Faith says, "We hope to be able to endure all things." Matthew 10:22 records Jesus' words: "He that endureth to the end shall be saved." As we endure there will be blue days. There might even be dark blue days, even a few black days in each life. There will be days spent kneeling and asking for solace, days spent searching the scriptures for support. There will be days when a priesthood blessing for strength is requested.

I trust Eve when she said with gladness, "Were it not for our transgression we never should have had seed, and never should have known good and evil." (Moses 5:11.) Opposition is the divine plan. Opposition is something to be glad about.

Navigating Through Life

Knowing there will be opposition does not make the hard times easier. During dark hours when I feel acted upon, I need to remember I am the one who charts my course through life. I stand at the helm and navigate. Under the watchful eye of a kind Father in Heaven, I must set the rudder so as not to drift aimlessly, tossed by the waves of self-pity or by winds that overwhelm. Montaigne said, "No wind favors him who has no destined port."

Alice asked the Cheshire cat, "Would you tell me, please, which way I ought to go from here?"

"That depends a good deal on where you want to get to," said the cat.

"I don't much care where—" said Alice.

"Then it doesn't matter which way you go," said the cat.

I must know where I am going, unless I want to end up somewhere else. If high self-esteem for myself and those I love is my destined port, and I look for a place on the map of life called self-esteem, I will not find it. Self-esteem is not a destination but rather the name of the sea-lane. If we are anchored to God's commandments, then high self-esteem is the process that takes us closer to him and his ways.

There are times I feel I am on an indirect course to no-where, that it doesn't much matter which way I go. I feel pressured to be so organized, so loving, so compassionate, and so positive that I don't want to set the sails or even mop the deck. When I am experiencing opposition, this is the time to stop and say, "Yes, I am stressed but I will not allow myself to send a distressed signal. I am in charge here."

Your Best Friend

As a modern nation we are concerned about pollutions factories put in the air, about corruptions TV and movies place in our minds, and about chemical contaminants we allow to enter our bodies. These are serious concerns. But more important than all of this is the mental pollution we put in our own minds when we continually think negatively about ourselves. We are experts at self-faultfinding, at self-putdowns, at dwelling on the bad and glossing over the good in ourselves. This is personal mind-pollution. Give yourself the same benefit you give others when you overlook their faults and praise their virtues. Keep your rose-colored glasses on when you look in the mirror.

As we look around at other mothers, it is easy to see the best and finest in them. Then we compare that seemingly perfect person with ourselves at our worst. It often appears that no one else has problems. But everyone does. Many of the problems are much worse than yours. Thoreau said most of us live lives of quiet desperation. Don't shackle your forward progress by negative thoughts. A healthy self-esteem needs positive thoughts to grow. Be your own best friend.

I hope the answer to the question "Is anyone out there building mother's self-esteem?" has been a resounding "Yes!"

You are building your own self-esteem. You are doing it by knowing that self-esteem isn't something that is packaged in a factory or synthesized in a laboratory. You are building your self-esteem by

1. knowing that motherhood can be difficult at times;

2. realizing that you and your children are in different cycles and that this season of life will pass;

3. learning techniques that will help in combatting mother abuse;

4. knowing self-esteem is a self-fulfilling prophecy;

5. adjusting to your marital status—married, divorced, or widowed;

6. having a plan to safeguard your emotional, physical, and spiritual self-esteem;

7. being willing to risk a little even though you are fearful because the potential for success outweighs the risk; and by

8. knowing that the ideas in this book are not new; you instinctively knew them all along. Self-esteem is sitting on your shoulder waiting to be invited in as a permanent part of your personality.

As Thyself

But you are not the only one who can build your self-esteem. I can hear you saying, "Hey, what goes? She has just spent a whole book telling me that if I don't build my own self-esteem, no one else will either." You are right, but there is someone else who can and probably will. I am not speaking of Heavenly Father, who we already know wants us to succeed and helps us daily. No, this person (or persons) is human and still can help.

Now that your curiosity has peaked, let me give you a few clues. Who understands the plight of a widow best? Who knows the depth of suffering a divorcée goes through? Who understands the abuse a mother of teenagers endures? Of course! The answer is another widow, another divorcée, or another mother of teenagers. So this is who can help to build your self-esteem—other mothers, like yourself, who can relate as no other can to your specific season of life.

Women can be their own support network. One woman can dry another's tears and be another's temporary crutch. I can sustain you. You can sustain me. Your smile, your kind word, your help when I need you, your pat on my back, my commitment never to gossip about you and yours to never gossip about me, will bless me as nothing else can.

I view the Relief Society as a self-esteem-building organization. Who better could help to build my self-esteem than a sister in the gospel who has been there?

Last week in Relief Society we had a lesson entitled "Self-Esteem." At the conclusion of the lesson our teacher did something I've never seen done before. She said, "Will all the widows and divorcées stand." No one moved. She said it again. "Will all the widows and divorcées stand." One called out, "Are you serious?" "Yes," she said with a slight irritation in her voice. One by one the sisters began to stand. Finally about one-third of the sisters were standing.

Then our teacher, who is a divorcée herself, said, "Look around at us. Remember who we are. We are special people. We need you. Invite us to dinner. Ask if we have a ride to the temple or to Relief Society. And when your husband comes home late and is grouchy, just remember, no man is coming home to us."

She could have asked all the women to stand who were struggling with a wayward child, or those who were stressed over finances, or those who were fatigued because of the care their aging parents demanded. She could have identified any of the multitude of tests this life passes out. We all would have stood several times. She could have said about each of us, "Love this sister. She is special. Her needs are unique and specific. You can bless her life. You can help to build and maintain her self-esteem."

Jesus said, "Love thy neighbor as thyself." The

second part of the command is really the first. Love yourself so you can love your neighbor. When you are down, work on loving yourself and building your own self-esteem. When you are up, you can love your neighbor as yourself and help her build her self-esteem.

We can each bless another sister by saying through our actions and words, "I love you where you are right now. I love you just the way you are. Don't feel guilt over problems that come into your life. No matter how good you are, bad things can still happen. It is part of the plan. It does not mean God is punishing you; it does not mean you are a bad person. It means you, and all the rest of us, are living in a telestial world. I love you because you are you."

We Made It

Well, here we are. We made it to the last chapter and almost the last page of this book. It has been good for me and my self-esteem. I hope it has been good for you and yours. In this book we have discussed many ways to build your own self-esteem—ideas that can bring you up from depression. Let me call these ideas elevators.

A few months ago I was depressed about my relationship with one of our teenagers. I also had made commitments to too many things. I wasn't sleeping well and was at the moment caught up in what seemed to be my well-deserved depression. I was shopping in a department store, racing here and there from floor to floor, trying to meet several deadlines. Finally I knew I had to go home even though my errand wasn't done. I got on the elevator to go to the parking lot. In my confusion I thought I was on the third floor going to the first. Actually, I was already on the first floor. Before the elevator door closed, a lady stepped on with us. "Are you going up?" she asked. "No down," I said. She looked up to see what floor we were on. "No, you aren't," she smiled, "you are as down as you can get." "If only you knew how true that is," I replied. The humor of the situation lifted my spirits. When you get down, find an elevator back up. You see, I was actually on my way up and didn't even know it. Consider the promises given in the next two scriptures:

"When thou art in tribulation, and all these things are come upon thee, even in the latter days, if thou turn to the LORD thy God, and shalt be obedient unto his voice; (for the Lord thy God is a merciful God;) he will not forsake thee." (Deuteronomy 4:30-31.)

"There hath no temptation taken you but such as is common to man; but God is faithful, who will not suffer you to be tempted above that ye are able; but will with the temptation also make a way to escape, that ye may be able to bear it." (1 Corinthians 10:22.)

These two scriptures state a secret. Each woman must have the confidence in her Father in Heaven that he will not send more problems than she can bear. We must have the hope to keep trying, keep going, keep doing. Our confidence in Heavenly Father gives us hope and confidence in ourselves. Confidence in ourselves is high self-esteem. "I am a child of God. His promises are sure. Celestial glory will be mine, if I will but endure."

Why not become part of a new generation of Mormon mothers who respond not to pressure but to principle, and who see beauty not only in the world but also in themselves?

Be the best you can be. Climb your own ladder to the celestial kingdom—one rung at a time. Use your individual talents, aspirations, faults, and trials to mold a woman, a mother, who paces her running with her strength, her desires with reality, and who travels life's journey with high self-esteem.

Index